W9-BSF-815

SPARK

SPARK

How to Lead Yourself and
Others to Greater Success

ANGIE MORGAN
COURTNEY LYNCH
AND SEAN LYNCH

Houghton Mifflin Harcourt
BOSTON   NEW YORK   2017

Copyright © 2017 by Lead Star, LLC

All rights reserved

For information about permission to reproduce selections from
this book, write to trade.permissions@hmhco.com or to Permissions,
Houghton Mifflin Harcourt Publishing Company, 3 Park Avenue,
19th Floor, New York, New York 10016.

www.hmhco.com

Library of Congress Cataloging-in-Publication Data
Names: Morgan, Angie, author. | Lynch, Courtney, author. |
Lynch, Sean, author.
Title: Spark : how to lead yourself and others to greater success /
Angela Morgan, Courtney Lynch, Sean Lynch.
Description: Boston : Houghton Mifflin Harcourt, 2017.
Identifiers: LCCN 2016002264 | ISBN 978-0-544-71618-6 (hardback) |
ISBN 978-0-544-71623-0 (ebook) | Subjects: LCSH:
Leadership. | Motivation (Psychology) | BISAC: BUSINESS &
ECONOMICS / Leadership. | BUSINESS & ECONOMICS /
Motivational. | BUSINESS & ECONOMICS / Management.
Classification: LCC HD57.7 .M6634 2016 | DDC 658.4/092 — dc23
LC record available at http://lccn.loc.gov/2016002264

Book design by Kelly Dubeau Smydra

Printed in the United States of America
DOC 10 9 8 7 6 5 4 3 2 1

Johari Window, page 25: After a design by Lead Star. © 2016 Houghton
Mifflin Harcourt Publishing Company. *Maslow's pyramid, page 129:*
© 2016 Houghton Mifflin Harcourt Publishing Company.

For my parents, Marilyn and Jerry Judge
— Angie

To my children, Jessica, Kara, and Brady,
who give me reason to Spark
— Courtney

To Vera, Connor, and Caitlin — you inspire me
— Sean

CONTENTS

FOREWORD

O UR MOST VALUABLE ASSET at FedEx is our culture. Of course, it's not a line item listed on our balance sheet, but it's genuinely tangible nonetheless. Our culture forms the foundation of the daily exchanges individual team members have with each other, our partners, and our customers. It encourages our leaders to lead by example and demonstrate the principles of commitment and teamwork. We know we're not just moving boxes around the globe. People depend upon us to deliver their lifesaving medicines, e-commerce items, and one-of-a-kind artifacts. We take that responsibility seriously, and our Purple Promise is a direct reflection of its importance: *We will make every FedEx experience outstanding.*

You don't just happen upon organizational excellence. Our culture was purpose-built, one leader at a time. And its design began with a great deal of inspiration from the finest leadership academy in the world: the United States military.

I became a Marine in 1966 after graduating from Yale University, and the leadership principles I learned in the Corps have been of incalculable value to me. Most business schools don't break down leadership the way the Marine Corps does. The teachers I found in the Corps, such as Staff Sergeant Richard Jackson and Gunnery Sergeant Allen Sora, were the most competent and courageous individuals I've ever met. And each one helped teach me that leadership isn't about authority. It's about building credible influence with others.

During my two tours in Vietnam, where I was responsible for leading a group of Marines who had very different backgrounds, perspectives, and life experiences than my own, I had the opportunity to apply every leadership principle the Corps taught me (principles I can still recite from memory to this day). These principles were very effective at helping me create a team in a highly volatile, demanding environment.

Though I took off the uniform nearly fifty years ago, there's no doubt the Corps left its mark on my life. My experience as a Marine imbued me with the confidence to revisit an idea I had envisioned during college — a business concept centered on an integrated air and ground delivery system. From there, FedEx was born.

Being an entrepreneur and getting an innovative venture off the ground certainly involves risk. But I was fortunate because the military had given me perspective on risk, which allowed me to have a high tolerance for ambiguity in those early days.

My experience as a Marine officer also allowed me to recognize that FedEx had the potential to exceed my expectations if we invested in our team's leadership development. Whether it was equipping our managers with the right skill sets or succession planning to ensure future managers would be ready to lead, we intentionally built a people-oriented culture. We believe that when people are placed first, they are positioned to provide the highest possible level of service. Profits are sure to follow.

Indeed, diligently building our team members' leadership skills has prepared us to be able to respond rapidly to changing market conditions, demonstrate agility amid uncertainty, and weather critical organizational change.

There is no doubt in my mind that if you were to visit FedEx's

Leadership Institute, you'd see the Marine Corps DNA in our culture. And I believe more businesses today could benefit by sharing proven leadership principles with professionals for use at all stages of their career. Leadership development efforts tap into every single team member's discretionary effort — *the level of effort people could give if they wanted to.* Unfortunately, too many organizations manage people in a way that ensures they do only what they must to get by. And the difference between these two performance levels is potentially millions of dollars.

The concept of leadership is not a difficult one to understand. It's simply about taking care of others and treating them fairly, communicating in a way that lets others know what they must do to be successful, and passing along praise for a job well done. It's that straightforward, but it's by no means intuitive. It must be learned and practiced.

Spark will help you do just that. The following pages detail the leadership behaviors that any professional, at any level, in any organization, can adopt to be a stronger leader. The authors, all military Veterans, share their personal experiences here in learning and applying the same leadership principles I was taught in 1966 — enduring principles that are still being taught today. These principles have been tried in the most chaotic of environments — with your commitment, you can test them in yours. Your ability to lead — *whether that's yourself, your team, or your organization* — will make the difference in the results you experience for years to come.

Frederick W. Smith
Chairman and CEO
FedEx Corporation

SPARK

INTRODUCTION: DEFINING A SPARK

A SPARK IS ALL ABOUT CHANGE.

Sparks are people who recognize that they don't have to accept what's given to them. They can do things differently to create the change they'd like to see. Their actions can directly shape their future, and they can make things better.

A Spark is also a moment when you realize that you have the ability to be a part of the solution you seek. You don't have to wait around for someone to create opportunities for you. You can create them yourself.

When Sparks are ignited, they're a catalyst for personal and organizational change. They're the individuals who have the courage to stand up and say, "We don't have to do things like we've always done them. We can do things better." They then cultivate the fortitude and temperament to lead themselves and others toward the results they seek.

Sparks aren't defined by the place they hold on an organizational chart; in fact, they exist throughout organizations. They're defined by their actions, commitment, and will, not by job titles. They're the ones who say, "I'll lead this," "I'll take responsibility," or, "This is tough, but we'll get it done." And then they follow through.

Sparks are hard to pinpoint during job interviews; their résumés might not convey their ingenuity and perseverance. They also don't always stand out in organizations. They may not fit into the right mold or have the right pedigree to be identified as "talent," yet their efforts are the reason great ideas get implemented, organizational change efforts take hold, and employee retention is strong.

Our world needs Sparks now more than ever.

The workplace reality is that the rate of change, the emergence of technology, shifting workforce demographics, and industry disruptions have created a VUCA environment: Volatile, Uncertain, Complex, and Ambiguous. All three of us heard this acronym when we served in the military, and now we are fascinated by how often business professionals use the same term to describe their working experience.

The military helped us confront VUCA by investing thousands of hours in building our leadership skills; that training transformed us into Sparks and helped us develop the inner confidence, commitment, and drive to see results through at all costs. Most professionals don't get access to this type of leadership development, however, and are left at a disadvantage when faced with challenge and change.

Many businesses seek to develop their teams by starting with hard skills and competencies, while reserving leadership skills for the management ranks. When they turn to leadership development, they typically use a curriculum that consists of coaching, communication, and project management skills in one- or two-day courses. These topics are important, but they are events — not processes — and they fail to develop individuals' capacity to learn and apply the behaviors that grant influence, inspire others, and drive results.

Furthermore, what gets lost in this approach is the opportunity to create organizational agility. Long gone are the days when one leader — or a select few leaders — called all the shots. As businesses become more global and matrices change reporting relationships, organizations need to decentralize decision-making and depend on individual contributors to get the job done. Without the proper development, these individuals can be stymied and initiatives can get stalled.

Organizations need leaders at all levels who will ensure that Sparks — and those with Spark potential — have the ability to create impact.

Our society values leadership — craves it, for that matter. Yet we don't teach it in formal education. Some of the most prestigious colleges and universities guarantee that their programs will make students into leaders, but the reality is that they don't offer leadership courses or even the experiences to make leadership development possible. A certificate or degree doesn't make you a leader. *You* make you a leader. And when you demonstrate leadership behaviors, you become a Spark.

If you are determined to take charge of your career and lead yourself and others to a better place, this book is for you. This book is also for business managers who want to drive performance in their organization by rethinking their approach to talent. Rather than identifying select individuals for development, they want to see all individuals working to their fullest ability.

Spark details behavior-based leadership practices that give any professional, at any level, the opportunity to flourish. In *Spark*, you'll learn about the key elements of leadership — character, credibility, accountability, vision, service, and confidence — and how to express them consistently.

Sparks are essential to the growth of any organization; once identified, they can be encouraged and positioned for success. If given the right setting and opportunities, Sparks can truly make all the difference in your organization. And if you're a Spark and have the courage to forge ahead, you will find yourself on a very fast track.

Becoming a Spark is a choice, and one that begins with rethinking how you respond to the most pressing challenges you're facing. Do you submit to them, assuming that you can't possibly do anything about them? Do you approach them the same way you always have, expecting to get a different result? Or do you take a stance and lead? Think carefully before you answer these questions, because your response could change everything — for you, for the people who depend on you, and for your organization.

LEADERSHIP INDOCTRINATION

Sean's Story

I learned how to lead right after I made some of the most important, but difficult, decisions of my life: dropping out of engineering school at Yale, switching my major to philosophy, and joining the Air Force after graduation.

My parents were outraged. "We're spending all this money on an Ivy League education and you're studying philosophy and going into the military?" My friends thought I was nuts: "We're going to get rich on Wall Street while you're going to be training in some desert? What's wrong with you, Sean?"

In other words, I was getting zero affirmation from my environment that my decisions were good ones, but they felt right to me. For the first time in my life, I was pursuing goals that were aligned with my passions. And I was going to realize my childhood dream of becoming a fighter pilot.

After I graduated from college, I was shipped off to Officer Candidate School (OCS), where I was immediately indoctrinated into the Air Force culture. I kept hearing the phrase "leadership development" in the classroom, along with the words "accountability" and "integrity." These were obviously important concepts to the Air Force, but ones I had never really thought much about. It was now becoming clear on a daily basis, however, that "accountability" and "integrity" were expectations that the Air Force fully embraced and that I had to meet. I still didn't understand what being a leader meant, though I soon would.

After I graduated from OCS, I was sent to flight school. I finally felt like I had arrived! One of the very first things I did in training was get in the backseat of an F-16 so I could become familiar with the Viper and learn more about piloting an aircraft. There are truly no words to describe the pure excitement I felt that morning as I was putting on my flight suit.

When I arrived at the hangar, I met with the pilot who would be flying the jet. He was a crusty old major who was also going to serve as my teacher for the day. I could tell that he took his job seriously just by his direct way of speaking to me, while giving me plenty of details about the sortie we were going out on. His instruction was interesting, but I have to admit that my focus was really more on the joy ride coming up.

When we took off, the speed took my breath away. And then there was turning, burning, airplanes whizzing by, and constant radio traffic. The squadron was simulating an attack on an airfield, and man, it was awesome. I was hanging on to the tail of the airplane for the entire ninety-minute flight!

When we landed, all the pilots, including the major and me, went into the "ready room" — a debriefing room where we discussed every detail of the sortie and pinpointed all of the lessons learned. Everyone was re-creating the event on whiteboards, and we were watching videos of each pilot's performance. I was lost during this discussion, which consisted mostly of acronyms that made sense to others but sounded like alphabet soup to me. But what captured my attention was the level of candor among the pilots.

Junior officers pointed out where their bosses made mistakes, and senior officers were open to their input and even asked for additional constructive criticism. I wasn't expecting this type of candid feedback in a rank-oriented culture. But it was clear that everyone in the squadron — not just the major, the highest-ranking officer in the room — felt compelled to address the squadron's performance and where it had fallen short.

At the end of the debriefing, when everyone started walking out, the major singled me out and asked me to stay. Surprised, I stopped in my tracks. He pointed his finger at me and then let me have it. "Hey, Lieutenant, how come you had nothing to add to that conversation? I didn't hear one word from you. You were out there. You saw what happened. Why didn't you speak up?" When I tried to jump in to defend myself and say that I was new, that I didn't know, that I was simply trying to learn, he quickly silenced me by saying, "The Air Force doesn't owe you anything, Lieutenant! Stop with the excuses, start contributing. You're new, but you're not dumb. Now, get out of here . . . and get a haircut!"

As I left the hangar, I could feel my face getting red from embarrassment. And when I got into my car, those emotions were suddenly replaced with anger. *What's wrong with the Air Force? Don't they know what I gave up to be here? I left a safe career path that was sure to lead to tremendous wealth. And now I'm stuck here in this stupid organization that treats its newest members like dirt. What's up with that major? Who does he think he is? He can't possibly believe he's teaching anyone by ranting and raving like he just did. What a poor excuse for an officer.*

But on my drive home, as my anger cooled, I started to turn

on myself. Maybe it wasn't the Air Force. Maybe it wasn't the major. Maybe it was me. Everyone in the debriefing room had seemed comfortable during the heated exchanges. Why couldn't I accept criticism? Why didn't I ask questions? Why didn't I contribute during the debriefing? The major was right — I might have been new, but I wasn't dumb. Maybe I didn't have what it took to succeed here. Maybe I did make the wrong choice.

I spent the better portion of the day cycling through the emotions of indignation, humiliation, shame, and despair. But by that night I had arrived at clarity. I had a choice: I could take the feedback I'd just heard and learn from it, or I could ignore it. If I chose to ignore it, I could envision a very frustrating future in the Air Force ahead of me. I had signed a six-year contract to serve, so I couldn't quit.

This was the moment when I realized that I needed to do something differently, something that I'd never done before, to overcome the situation I found myself in. In short, this was my Spark moment.

Up until this point in my career, if I came across a problem, simple hard work solved it. Difficult class? Study more. Preparing for a swim meet? Train more. Need money for college? Get a part-time job. But my old-fashioned work ethic wasn't going to solve this problem. I needed to figure out how to lead, starting with myself.

I knew I didn't want to waste time fighting the Air Force culture, but I could change my response to it. This was my time to make a conscious effort to override my reaction to the situation and apply the leadership lessons my trainers at OCS had talked about. Accountability and integrity? Yeah, I needed those. Several weeks earlier, in the sterile classroom environment, leadership hadn't sounded too complicated. But during this moment of insecurity, being a leader was suddenly incredibly challenging. I had to be better than my instincts, all of which were directing me toward negative, self-defeating, irresponsible actions that might protect my ego but weren't going to help me succeed in the Air Force.

In this moment, I had to come to grips with my reality. The major was right. I had just been presented with a learning opportunity, but I was disengaged from the lesson. My focus had been on the thrill of the jet ride, but it should have been on my responsibility to contribute to the team. Moving forward, I would make a point of speaking up, even if I felt afraid of asking a stupid question.

I also knew that I was going to have to learn how to take professional criticism. I'd just sat through a debriefing with talented fighter pilots at the peak of their game. When they received feedback, they didn't get defensive or offer excuses, as I'd done. They welcomed criticism and appreciated it — something that I was going to have to be able to do.

The major's criticism couldn't have come at a better time in my career. When I was able to separate my emotions from his message and apply the leadership lessons I learned at OCS, I grew as a professional. This unexpected and painful experience prepared me for the inevitable feedback I faced later on in flight school, in the squadrons where I served, in my career at Delta Airlines, and now at Lead Star. I also learned how to deliver feedback to others in a way that helped improve the teams and organizations I've been a part of. Excellence and high performance happen only when everyone on the team — not just a select few — chooses to lead.

That's the value of Spark behavior. It doesn't matter whether you're a major or a lieutenant, a CEO or an administrative assistant. You only need one Spark to ignite a high-impact change in an organization, even if the first person to change is yourself.

That may be all your company needs to achieve significant and noticeable improvement.

IT'S NOT ABOUT THE JOB TITLE

Angie's Story

We recognize that when you, like many professionals, experience challenges in your work environment, such as conflict with a colleague or a lost sales opportunity, you might not think immediately, *How am I going to be a leader in this situation?* That's because most people think of leadership as a title, not as a set of behaviors, so they don't see themselves as leaders capable of applying leadership to their challenges. At Lead Star, we define a leader as *someone who influences outcomes and inspires others.* You can be a manager without being a leader. The reverse is also true. You can be a leader without being a manager.

Sean, Courtney, and I all learned about leadership during our time in the military. Whereas Sean learned in the Air Force, Courtney and I learned about leadership in the Marine Corps. There are many differences between the services, which we joke about all the time, but there are also many strong similarities in how they go about developing leaders.

Courtney and I acquired hundreds of hours of experiential leadership training during our six-month infantry course, The Basic School (TBS). Here we were assigned roles in which we were responsible for leading our peers, but without rank. In other words, we couldn't say, "Do this because I'm the boss," when working with our colleagues.

Peer leadership, as you probably know, is one of the most challenging types of leadership because your peers can and will push back without fear of repercussion. If they don't agree with a decision you make, there is no silent protest — you'll hear about it immediately. When you screw up, the jokes that would typically be told behind your back are told right to your face. In short, learning peer leadership skills certainly kept us on our toes, but afterward we had a clear view of our strengths and weaknesses.

This training had a specific purpose: to ensure that when we got to the "real" Marine Corps to lead a platoon, we wouldn't have to rely on our rank or position to be effective but would have learned how to lead through influence.

Once we were in the Corps, it was apparent that everyone, from the junior-most Marine to the most senior, learned the exact same leadership skills. We also all viewed ourselves as leaders and were expected to apply these skills to our role, regardless of whether that was leading ourselves, a fire team of four, or many more. The leadership concepts never changed — only the application of these concepts as responsibilities increased.

While in the military, Courtney, Sean, and I lived and breathed leadership every day. So you can imagine our surprise when we left active duty and started working in the private sector. We met great people, but so many of them had not been introduced to leadership in a practical way. This was evident in the little things, like the prevalence of placing blame, not following through on commitments, and saying one thing but doing another. These behaviors were tolerated in the private sector, and in some circumstances socially acceptable, but in the military such behaviors inevitably cost lives. Another surprise for us was working with managers who were expected to be leaders but had never been prepared for that responsibility. They were solid individual contributors, but they struggled with figuring out how to let go of doing everything themselves and start leading their teams.

The bottom line is twofold: Leadership is probably one of the most misunderstood concepts in our society. And to many people, leadership is only about bosses or supervisors — about people in power.

I remember working with a colleague on my sales team in the pharmaceutical industry who was a great communicator, had amazing educational credentials, and knocked her sales quota out of the park every quarter. Our clients loved her, our team valued her, and new hires wanted to be like her. I once shared my respect with her: "I'm so glad you're on my team. You do a great job leading us." She corrected me quickly. "Well, I'm not the leader, I'm just your colleague," she said. "But I hope to be a leader one day."

In other words, she was a Spark. But she didn't recognize it.

Courtney was having similar experiences working as an attorney in Washington, DC. She met so many talented lawyers who didn't consider themselves leaders, even though they were bringing in millions of dollars of revenue for their firm, delegating responsibilities to associates, mentoring junior attorneys new to their firm, creating networking events for current and prospective clients, and serving on nonprofit boards in their communities.

Why did they not realize they were leaders? It was puzzling. In our eyes, these men and women were Sparks! They were the ones initiating action and creating conditions for success, both their own and that of others. Why were they not making that connection? We concluded that many professionals believe that if they aren't in the very top position on the organizational chart or haven't been named the head of their team, they don't see themselves as leaders.

To us, this belief clearly represented a missed opportunity for everyone — for individuals as well as for their organization.

INSPIRING MORE SPARKS

These observations inspired Courtney and me to create our company Lead Star in 2004 and to coauthor our first book, *Leading from the Front,* which translates hard-core Marine Corps principles into leadership lessons for use by business professionals. We began with a simple goal: to help top-level professionals understand leadership fundamentals that work. But as our firm grew, our work evolved toward helping organizations design programs to inspire Sparks at all levels of their organization — from the frontline leaders *all* the way up to C-suite personnel.

Our work has brought us inside many well-known organizations, including Facebook, Accenture, Marathon Oil, Boston Scientific, Best Buy, and the United Way, as well as lesser-known — but equally as impressive — smaller businesses, nonprofits, and government agencies. And we've witnessed what happens when individuals start to view themselves as leaders. They Spark! Suddenly they don't feel hemmed in by their place in the corporate hierarchy as they realize that they can have greater influence over their circumstances. They start to understand that they can take the initiative to navigate through some of the complex challenges they are experiencing. They also choose to stop waiting around for someone else to direct them; instead, they start taking action where action is needed.

Spark is the culmination of our collective years in business. It's all about the active change you can take to be a leader, no matter what your title or position. In this book, we're going to provide you with behavior-based leadership practices steeped in research so that you can Spark too. We're also going to share with you plenty of stories of other Sparks so that you can gain encouragement and inspiration from their actions and results.

THE TIME IS NOW

Our world isn't slowing down. We work in a knowledge economy, and there's a premium for leaders who can rise above the noise to take on new challenges and drive results. Although no one can slow the universe down so that everyone can catch up, there is one thing that all of us can do — in fact, *must do* — to gain control of our circumstances. *We must lead.*

Many organizations are now facing the reality that to thrive in the face of workplace challenges they need leadership from their entire team — top-down, side-to-side, and bottom-up. Only with Sparks throughout the organization can they keep pace with the many changes they are implementing to be competitive.

We've observed businesses updating their facilities, implementing lean processes, and working diligently on their global supply chains, but overlooking the most critical variable: *their people.* By providing out-of-date incentives, failing to offer competitive wages, and not providing sufficient training and development, they're effectively cultivating an antiquated workforce for their innovative product. Sure, these businesses lower costs, but in the end they're shortchanging their talent. The workforce practices of a bygone era cannot meet twenty-first-century demands.

As organizations become less title-centric and more focused on identifying and developing Sparks at every level, the results they experience are immediate. We've witnessed it. Thanks to Sparks within their ranks, companies respond more rapidly to changing market conditions because they've become more nimble, and their employees become more engaged because they've realized that they can effect change. Moreover, these companies attract the talented people who are seeking out workplace cultures that encourage employees to thrive.

THE COURAGE TO LEAD

Our goal with *Spark* is to share with you those actions you need to take to become a leader in your environment. And because we firmly believe that a leader has a responsibility to develop those around him or her, we conclude each chapter with precise suggestions and ideas on how you can inspire others to begin their Spark journeys too. We'll also share with you some common blind spots that leaders have, so that you can become aware of what you might be doing that is unintentionally affecting your ability to influence and inspire.

Leadership skills, like all skills, take time to develop. They are not innate. None of us are born leaders; we're made into leaders. Your self-development begins with developing the courage to lead. What we learned in the military is that courage isn't the absence of fear — it's the ability to take action in the face of fear.

One of your first acts of courage might be to recognize that leadership development is going to make you uncomfortable. We're going to be asking you to build new habits, which can be hard to do. The results, though, are worth your efforts.

1

CONFRONTING THE MYTHS
OF LEADERSHIP

To be a Spark, you have to recognize yourself as a leader. Know the pathway to leadership development and commit yourself to it. You're not chosen to be a leader. You choose to lead.

B ECOMING A SPARK REQUIRES first recognizing that you, like anyone else, have the potential to be a leader. Unfortunately, however, many would-be leaders are held back by myths about who and what a leader is. You're limiting your leadership potential if you buy into one or all of these three commonly held — but erroneous — notions of leadership:

- Leaders are born.
- Leaders trust their instincts.
- A title makes you a leader.

These ideas are perpetuated in our society and have been adopted in some of the world's best-known organizations. Many people believe that leadership is somehow a birthright, or that leadership is a gut feeling, or that you become a leader when you finally get that promotion.

These beliefs are flat-out wrong.

The best way to challenge the myths around leadership is

to follow the science and see where it leads us. You'll realize quickly that leadership isn't an exclusive designation reserved for the exceptional and privileged few. Being a Spark is an act of free will, and when you start to make the behavioral choices consistent with being a Spark, you will see what you can do (versus what you can't do) in your environment. You'll also gain the influence necessary to create the change you'd like to see and become the person with whom everyone wants to work. More importantly, you'll be leading through *influence,* not through title, and that makes a big, big difference.

LEADERS AREN'T BORN — THEY'RE MADE

Courtney's Story

I'm 100 percent proof positive that leaders aren't born. Sure, my parents gave me some quality DNA, but my journey to becoming a Spark began when I sensed that something was missing from my life. I wasn't sure what it was, but I realized that I needed to turn inward to find it.

I was an entrepreneur long before I started my first company, Lead Star. I just had a gift for making things happen. Some of my initiatives were good, and some ... well, not so much. For example, as a kid I once devised a moneymaking scheme that involved selling tickets to a prizeless raffle. I may not have always demonstrated the best integrity in my youth, but I guess you could at least say I had a knack for ingenuity and inventiveness.

As I grew older I found that I had a developing sense of confidence in my ability to create opportunities. From succeeding in college and getting exciting internships to landing competitive jobs in journalism, I found myself experiencing success at a pretty fast rate. But despite these accomplishments, something about my success just didn't feel right. Shortly after college, when I was working in television news, I found myself at a personal crossroads.

My achievements weren't fulfilling, and I was searching for something more meaningful. I couldn't name it then, but looking back I know exactly what it was: I was seeking a transformative experience that would help me grow and develop beyond the skills and abilities I was born with — to go beyond the knowledge I had gathered in college.

This personal search for "more" led me to explore other career paths that had interested me as a kid. Having grown up in the Washington, DC, area, I had always been fascinated by the men and women in the military. Two of my friends' fathers had served, and I admired and respected them. So one day I stopped by the Marine Corps recruiter's office to learn more. The recruiter didn't try to sell me on the Corps; instead, he asked me if I was ready for the challenge of a lifetime. He must have seen me coming from a mile away. "Absolutely! Tell me more," I said. Before too long I was signing a contract and preparing for Marine Corps training.

My family and friends were pretty surprised that I had chosen to join the military, let alone the Marines. They knew I loved adventure but never thought I'd channel my love for challenge into such a dramatic career choice. My parents were nervous about my decision, especially when they considered the possibility that I could be sent into harm's way, but extremely proud and supportive. But before I could wear the uniform, I had to make it through training.

Now, when most people think of Marine Corps training, they think of the intense physicality of the experience, but what was most profound for me was the character-building process I underwent. Marine Corps training held me to the highest of standards, forced me to subordinate my own personal needs to those of the greater group, and pushed me past the point of physical exhaustion to a place where I had to rely on mental endurance to keep going. And whenever I started to experience self-doubt, I had instructors or fellow officer candidates who encouraged me to push even harder. It was during those dark, quiet moments when I truly felt I had nothing left that I started to discover the "more" that I had been craving.

For the first time in my life, I came face to face with my limitations, but I also discovered an inner resolve I never knew existed. I had to struggle with my ego, which was real, powerful, and dangerous and would often prevent me from practicing the self-confrontation necessary to overcome my weaknesses. I also realized that to succeed in the Corps I couldn't do it alone. Most of my training was designed to be experienced with a team. I soon realized, too, that any success I could experience with a team would be more significant than anything I could do by myself.

Overall, I consider myself an accidental leader: I stumbled upon my leadership development experience by walking into a recruiter's office and declaring I was up for a challenge. So, yes, I know that, considering how it happened, I'm a "made" leader. But the science that supports my belief that anyone can be a "made" leader is pretty fascinating.

Researchers from the Minnesota Center for Twin and Family Research have studied identical twins separated at birth to explore the question of whether leaders are born or made. Their work has led them to a conclusion that makes total sense: that we're born with about 30 percent of our leadership abilities, including qualities like intelligence, extroversion, and good looks. For example, imagine you're in a meeting and someone rattles off a brilliant idea. Influenced by that person's intellect and ability to think quickly, you then offer your take on that inspired idea. What this means is that this person has effectively led you — by influencing you and inspiring you.

Or imagine that you're at a conference and the keynote speaker is bouncing off the walls with raw energy. (Tony Robbins, anyone?) You're moved and inspired by the speaker's passion and conviction. Again, in this moment you have been led.

The same is true for attractive people. You might not have been around for the first televised presidential debate in 1960, when a relaxed and tanned John F. Kennedy squared off against a tired, gaunt, and poorly shaved Richard Nixon. Whereas radio listeners declared Nixon the winner, the 70 million television viewers who had been able to ogle JFK disagreed overwhelmingly. So, yes — we're naturally swayed by someone's good looks.

The fact that you're reading a book on leadership because you care about your career is a strong indicator that you hit the "born into leadership" jackpot. You have solid, innate leadership tendencies. But remember, that's only 30 percent of the equation. Don't spend too much time trying to improve the qualities you were born with, since they can't be changed much, if at all. Instead, redirect your efforts toward the other 70 percent — the Spark qualities you can develop, just as I did in the Corps. The truth is, prior to learning to lead, I had never focused on developing leadership behaviors. I didn't even know what they were because I had never been introduced to them.

The "made" leadership behaviors we promote are attainable by any committed person, in any environment. Spark qualities include being credible to others so that they trust you, holding yourself accountable to your challenges, making good decisions when you're feeling pressure to act, expressing your confidence in clutch moments, and bringing a group of individuals together to form a full and cohesive team.

When you think about any of these Spark qualities, you start to realize that they represent ways in which you can consciously choose to behave. However, these choices are easier to understand than to carry out, because they require that you defy human nature. This leads us to the next myth about leadership — that leaders trust their instincts. As you'll see, your instincts first need to be challenged before they can be trusted.

LEADERS CHALLENGE THEIR INSTINCTS

Too often in business we hear the phrase "trust your instincts." Unfortunately, that's not always the best advice, because our instincts aren't always consistent with Spark behavior. When we avoid conflict, overreact to bad news, or procrastinate on decisions, we're acting on our instincts and not influencing our environment. We're simply *reacting*, which puts us at a disadvantage.

The way to stop reacting and start responding like a Spark is to invoke higher-order cognitive processes to control your actions. What does this mean when it comes to leadership development? Get inside your head and start paying attention to your reactions to challenging situations. The two most important processes to take notice of are cognitive flexibility and cognitive discipline, which help you get off autopilot — where your basic instincts reside — and consciously respond to challenging situations in an inspiring, influential, and well-thought-out way.

Cognitive flexibility is commonly described as the ability to switch your thinking in order to solve problems, which we all do really well with the non-people-related challenges we experience. "This machine's not working, so let's get a workaround." "We're 10 percent short of our quota, so let's start brainstorming marketing activities that will help us make up the difference." "The caterer didn't show up for the meeting, so let's call for pizza."

But do we apply the same style of creative problem-solving when it comes to the people (and people problems) we encounter daily? Chances are, no. Or at least, not always.

We all fall into ruts and routines with people, especially in long-standing relationships, and there are times when we don't flex in our approach when dealing with tough situations. This can lead to roadblocks, which limit the level of leadership we provide others.

A colleague of ours once shared that her breakthrough leadership moment came when she realized that she couldn't change others but she could change herself in order to improve a relationship with a coworker. She'd been working with Mike for more than five years when she realized that their relationship was in a very bad place. Whenever they partnered together on projects, there was tension and friction, so much so that their work product was impacted and their manager was frustrated. "Why can't you two get along?" he challenged them both. In her mind, the answer was obvious: *Mike's defensive when he gets feedback, he's stubborn and unwilling to listen to other people's ideas, and he's volatile with his emotions.* As soon as she rolled out that list of excuses in her mind, she had a thought: *I wonder what Mike would say about me?* She spent time considering her style from Mike's point of view, and it didn't take her too long to realize that there were things she did to aggravate him, which further damaged their relationship.

For one, when she gave him feedback, she did so directly, without much tact. *It's no wonder he doesn't take it well,* she thought. She also realized that she could be stubborn with her ideas too, and she reasoned that this could be infuriating to others.

After this period of reflection, she made a conscious effort to focus on delivering thoughtful, helpful feedback and listening more to others' viewpoints before stating hers. These small adjustments in her approach to Mike transformed their relationship, which genuinely surprised her. "I never knew that such small actions on my part could have such a positive impact. Before I took some time to reconsider my approach, no one in our firm wanted to work on a project with Mike and me because we were so alienating to others. Now people are actually asking to partner up with us."

And that's the type of impact cognitive flexibility can have.

The first step in solving people problems is recognizing that you don't have to stay on the well-worn path you're used to, getting the (unsatisfactory) results you've always gotten. You can Spark by purposely choosing to change your approach.

A key second step is demonstrating *cognitive discipline:* the ability to inhibit an instinctual or habitual reaction and substitute a more effective, less obvious response instead — a Spark response.

Here's how it works. Imagine that you're co-presenting at a meeting, and your colleague throws you under the bus. Internally, you're hopping mad because you think the failure is on him: he was never clear on what he wanted, he never provided you with the data you needed, and he shouldn't be blaming you — he should be blaming himself. So what do you do in the moment when your instincts are telling you to fight, take flight, or freeze? Well, this is one of those instances when you need to avoid acting on your instincts. Instead, as Sean would tell you, you've got to "stop and wind the clock."

When he was learning how to fly a jet, Sean was taught that an instinctual response to an in-flight emergency would make him panic or act erratically, creating a dangerous situation for himself and his crew. Instead of reacting immediately to an emergency, he was first told to say to himself, *Stop and wind the clock.*

This was a metaphor for slowing down his thinking to respond calculatedly and intentionally to the situation, like accessing a mental checklist or starting to work through proper procedures. "Stop and wind the clock" is essentially the pilot's version of what we learned in elementary school when we were guided to "stop, drop, and roll" if our clothes were ever to catch on fire. So the next time you feel like you're about to act on your instincts, remember to first "stop and wind the clock" before you do. That can buy you the time necessary to exercise cognitive discipline and be the Spark you need to be by acting responsibly. Rather than allowing your emotions and instincts to determine your behavior, you'll be consciously choosing to engage your brain and its impressive problem-solving capabilities.

It should be apparent at this point that leadership development mostly happens above the shoulders. The next myth we have to address relates to timing: when does a person decide to lead?

IT'S YOUR CHOICE TO BE A LEADER

Many people think the only way to become a leader is to be a boss. But simply having a title has never, ever made anyone a leader. No one else can make or anoint you a leader. The only way to become a Spark is to *make yourself into one.* When you decide to become a Spark, you need to spend serious time reflecting on where you are on the leadership development continuum. What are your real strengths? What are your true weaknesses? This knowledge helps you recognize opportunities for your development.

One of the Marine Corps' top leadership principles is: "Know yourself and seek self-improvement." The Corps recognizes that its leaders are successful when they have real awareness of their talents and can put themselves in a position to leverage them. Leaders also need to be open to feedback that will allow them to shore up their weaknesses. A high level of candor between ourselves and others generates self-awareness.

The more self-aware we are as Sparks, the greater our ability to own our shortcomings and correct them before they affect others. For example, if you know that your impatience is off-putting to others, you can take a few deep breaths during meetings to manage your angst or practice active listening to focus on others' feelings and not your own. Or if you are aware that you lose focus easily, you can develop techniques that help you be more present. (Useful hint: get the cell phone off the table during meetings.) Tweaks like these to our leadership style help us cultivate the influence and inspiration necessary to be a Spark.

A useful model for developing this level of self-awareness is the Johari Window, which was developed in the 1950s by two psychologists, Joseph Luft and Harrington Ingham. According to this model, there are four aspects of awareness:

The first aspect of self-awareness is "what you know and everyone knows" about you. This aspect covers the truths about yourself that you have shared and that have become common knowledge among others. Maybe it is well known in your organization that you grew up in Nashville, went to Boston College, and own a chocolate lab puppy. Or, taking it deeper, maybe it's common knowledge that you love to talk ideas but not the details, or that you avoid conflict because heightened emotions make you uncomfortable. The more you share facts like these, the more transparent you are — and the more people are influenced by your openness and, likewise, feel more comfortable to

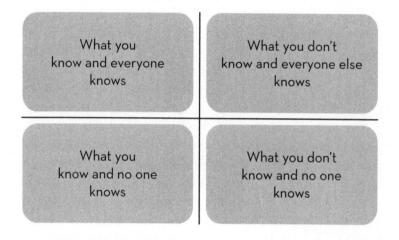

disclose information about themselves. This type of information exchange advances your relationships.

The next aspect of self-awareness is "what you know and no one knows" about you. These are our secrets, and while we'd never advise you to share all of your secrets at work, there might be key information you haven't shared that is holding you back from either accessing opportunities or building relationships. Maybe you want a promotion, but your boss doesn't know and therefore doesn't advocate for you. Or maybe you're caring for an elderly parent and are really struggling with this responsibility. You haven't confided this to anyone, though several of your colleagues have been in your position before. If you were to share this, you'd get access to their guidance and support, which could potentially help you in meaningful ways.

The next aspect is "what you don't know and no one knows" about you. We consider this quadrant "untapped potential." Maybe you have a knack for product development, have the potential to be a great writer, or have the raw talent of a world-class guitarist. But because you've never explored this area, neither you *nor others* have access to this hidden knowledge. As you make attempts to push yourself into new experiences and gain a greater appreciation for your strengths, weaknesses, and capabilities, you expand your self-awareness.

The final aspect of self-awareness is the gold mine: "what you don't know and everyone else knows" about you. Perhaps you're a poor communicator when you're overwhelmed, or maybe you're a micromanager when you delegate tasks. Maybe you hide out in your office too much and don't spend enough time on the production floor talking with your team members. Without access to your blind spots, it's difficult for you to improve upon them — and it may be precisely these blind spots that are holding you back from becoming an influential and inspirational leader to others.

As you keep reading and learning about Spark behaviors, we'd like to encourage you to use the Johari Window to help you evaluate your current performance against Spark standards. But don't just assess your strengths and weaknesses from *your* point of view; challenge yourself to consider the points of view of others, such as by asking yourself, *I personally think I'm good when it comes to credibility — but would my colleagues share that same opinion of me? What about my manager? What about my friends?* You might even develop the courage to ask them directly to help you expand your self-awareness. A simple tactic to facilitate this would be to send out an email to your manager, peers, direct reports, etc., saying, "I'm developing my leadership skills right now. I'd love your feedback. In a couple of days I'm going to stop by your office and I'd love to hear from you two things that I do well at my job and two areas where I could improve. It'd be great if you could share examples too." And when this feedback gives you information about areas where you could improve, don't get defensive; instead, thank those who responded to your request. After all, they've just given you a valuable gift.

Ironically, in a perfect world, the four aspects of the Johari Window shouldn't be balanced. When the first aspect — what you know and what everyone knows about you — is greater than the other three, you project a sense of openness and that builds trust. This means that you're open to sharing information about yourself and being vulnerable in your environment, that you engage in new experiences to try new things, and that you're open to the feedback of others. And as a Spark, when people trust you, they're willing to be led by you.

As you can tell, the Spark development process does require that you commit yourself to growth, which can be a fascinating — as well as uncomfortable — proposition for many people.

THE IMPORTANCE OF ONE'S MINDSET

Angie's Story

I've met too many professionals who, for whatever reason, fully believe that you can't teach an old dog new tricks. I disagree wholeheartedly, and research conducted by Professor Carol Dweck of Stanford University backs me up. Her results strongly suggest that learning and development stop only when we adopt a fixed mindset rather than a growth-oriented mindset. So, yeah, you can teach an old dog new tricks — *as long as the dog is willing to learn.* Dweck's research and subsequent book, entitled *Mindset,* shed some light on adult learning and how we unconsciously choose to stop seeking out challenges, thus limiting our opportunities for success. But we can also make a conscious choice to grow, which opens up a world of possibilities. I can personally attest to this.

I read *Mindset* at a pivotal moment in my career. Courtney and I had finally made it past the "Are we going to make it?" point in starting up Lead Star that every successful entrepreneur has to go through. We had diverse clients, steady work, and consistent paychecks. It was also evident to my friends, family, and colleagues that this Lead Star thing was working out, because they would ask me questions about what was next. What was our growth strategy? Did we need to hire more people in order to scale? Was acquisition by a larger company our exit strategy?

These were all great questions, but ones I didn't have answers to — not because I didn't think about my future, but because I didn't have an education to fall back on to help me make an informed decision. I was an English major who had served in the Marine Corps — I just didn't know enough about running a business to manage a company, let alone lead a company into a bigger future I couldn't yet picture.

Up until this point, Courtney and I had grown our business through hard work and moxie. That had gotten us pretty far, but now the stakes were higher. Our work was no longer simply providing leadership training. We were now becoming more consultative in our approach as more and more CEOs were making us their trusted advisers and sought out our insight on strategy, processes, and organizational structure. I wanted to provide better service to our clients, and I came to understand that meant I needed a formal business education.

The idea of graduate school wasn't a stretch for me. I had always wanted to go, but the *idea* of business school made me cower. I didn't think I could handle the academics because, frankly, I was bad at math. I dropped out of calculus in college after flunking my first test because I didn't want an F on my academic record. And in business school I would have to take accounting, finance, and statistics — real math-intensive courses.

I believed there was a serious chance I could fail, and I didn't want to suffer through that embarrassment at this stage of my career.

But fresh from reading *Mindset,* I thought more about my relationship with math and why I thought I was bad at it. Was this the truth — or was it something that someone told me and I unconsciously adopted as a belief? Just because I avoided math and preferred studying English didn't necessarily mean that I was bad at math, I reminded myself. Maybe I wasn't as bad with numbers as I thought. Maybe my struggle with calculus in college was just a mistake.

After researching different executive MBA programs and isolating the ones that didn't require a GMAT score (and thank goodness many don't, because that allowed me to delay my reunion with math as long as possible), I found the perfect program and applied. Not too long after, I received a letter from the University of Michigan's Ross School of Business that conveyed in the first paragraph that I was accepted into the program, but in the second paragraph informed me that there was a condition: I first had to pass a quantitative reasoning test because according to my college transcripts I had no math background. Apparently the admissions office also lacked confidence in my numerical abilities. This was discouraging, but as my husband pointed out, "Hey, if you can't pass the test, there is no way you belong in business school. In the long run, this test could save you time and money." (His logic was spot-on, but not appreciated in my moment of insecurity.)

To overcome the hurdle that was preventing me from being a student, I did what I've always done: I threw my work ethic at it. I studied, practiced math problems, and then studied some more. I would even bring my worksheets on plane rides when traveling to client sites, which would always prompt interesting comments from fellow passengers. "What are you doing? You look a little too old to be a high school student." What I learned was that I wasn't bad at math — it just took me more time to work through math problems. When I was an undergrad student, I hadn't had the patience — or the discipline and endurance — to learn what I was learning now.

After some serious focused effort, I took the test and passed. And then, twenty months later, I earned my MBA. What's more, I overcame a long-held faulty belief about myself and consequently got out of my own way. None of this would have happened if I hadn't checked my mindset, challenged a long-held assumption that my problem-solving abilities were limited, and made a conscious decision to be growth-oriented and to push my limits.

I've spent enough hours talking with successful, well-educated, and extremely sharp professionals to know that we all have our weaknesses and insecurities. But many of us don't spend enough time reflecting on whether our limitations are valid or self-imposed — are they real or just perceived? And many of us don't check our mindset to ensure that we're poised for development. When you take the time to challenge your assumptions, you might discover quickly that you have the talents necessary to take the next big leap that will lead you to your next level of success.

SPARK ACTIONS

In summary, on your Spark journey you must:

- Choose to lead. No one else makes you a leader. *You* make you a leader.
- Embrace the struggle within — instead of worrying about

what you weren't born with, build upon what you already have.

- Focus on responding, not reacting, to the people and events you encounter.
- Anticipate your blind spots — challenge yourself to gain a full view of your strengths and limitations.
- Be open to examining your beliefs about your abilities and exploring your hidden talents.

CHARGING AHEAD

Your Spark development begins when you opt into the process by rethinking what real leadership is and appreciating that you have really great raw material to work with. The next step — which requires self-awareness and the adoption of a growth mindset — is paying attention to your own thoughts, ideas, and behaviors in the workplace that either enhance or limit your influence. Here are a few activities you can find at www.sparks lead.us that will help you develop both self-awareness and a growth mindset:

- *Circle of Influence:* First, spend some time thinking about your key relationships — with friends, family members, colleagues, managers, and direct (or even indirect) reports. Consider your opportunities to lead within these relationships: how do you influence and inspire these individuals? This brief reflection exercise will get you thinking about your circle of influence and how you're already leading in many of your key relationships.
- *Self-Awareness:* Then consider your strengths and weaknesses. In one of our exercises at www.sparkslead.us, we

ask you questions that will help you both uncover the qualities that define you and reflect on how you can leverage your strengths in your environment.

- *Leader Discussion:* Finally, if you feel that your team would benefit from a refreshed version of "real leadership," we outline a group activity that you can lead to help your colleagues reimagine leadership and discuss how stronger leadership would improve your team.

You can grow and develop into a Spark. Once you've spent some time reflecting, you'll be ready to move on to the next chapter, which highlights one of the most important and essential Spark behaviors that you can develop — character. Being a person of sound character — someone whose values and actions are in alignment — is absolutely essential in your Spark journey.

2

YOUR CHARACTER: THE CONGRUENCE BETWEEN VALUES AND ACTIONS

By gaining awareness of what you truly value, you can think and act in ways that allow you to direct your life and have influence over others.

A LEADER, BY DEFINITION, has followers. But people will follow you only if they trust you.

Yep. We said it. *Trust.* The "T-word" makes some business professionals cringe. They become uncomfortable, not because they don't want trust in their workplace, but because developing it requires discussions involving feelings, emotions, and introspection — topics that make some folks squirm inside.

And yet figuring out how to be trustworthy and how to trust others can be critical for your own success and for that of your team. Never underestimate or discount the importance of trust.

When we were designing a nine-month leadership program for a Silicon Valley tech company, our client — the VP of ad sales — had just met some Special Forces service members and was most impressed by how everyone looked out for one another. She was adamantly convinced that most of her team's challenges would be solved if team members could demonstrate the "I've got your back" behaviors she'd observed. "How do they do that?" she asked.

"They trust each other," we replied.

"Trust?" she repeated. "Ugh. But that feels so squishy. I don't know how my team would respond to a course focused on trust."

Hey, we get it. Too often when people hear "leadership development" they think of trust falls, group hugs, and school circle moments. "Soft skills development" can seem like the ultimate touchy-feely exercise. Some people also become wary when leadership conversations center on concepts like character and values. These topics might seem uncomfortable, irrelevant, or unworthy of exploration in a business environment. Yet you can't be a Spark without a solid understanding of your values and how these manifest in your character, which determines whether or not people trust you.

We reassured the VP that a leadership program centered on character and led by former military service members wasn't going to involve rainbows and unicorns. Our focus in the program was first on *context* — creating the business case for trust — and then on *content* — detailing how individuals could contribute to a trustworthy team that delivered solid results.

The three of us had all gone through some profound development experiences ourselves, and those experiences, by raising our awareness of the role played by trust and character in our daily lives, helped shape the program's design.

THE CHARACTER LABORATORY

Angie's Story

Everyone has an image of what military training looks like, and Hollywood in particular has done a great job of portraying it. Among the most famous scenarios is Marine Corps boot camp, which has been rendered in many classic films. Having these film images in my head might explain why I was so nervous when it came time for me to head off to my own military train-ing. Having seen the movies, I was feeling like I knew a bit too much about what I was in for. And in fact, true to its reputa-tion, my Marine Corps training was tough. It came complete with countless push-ups, angry drill instructors, and endless marches.

Prospective officers attend something similar to boot camp — it's called Officer Candidate School (OCS), the first official program you have to pass before earning the title "Marine." At OCS, I knew I was being screened to see if I had the physical and mental endurance necessary to lead Marines in combat, but I didn't realize that was only part of the evaluation process. They were also looking to see if I was a good fit for their culture, which was steeped in Marine Corps values, history, and tradi-tion.

Each day was a challenge. We were woken up at 5:00 a.m., pushed through classes and physical exercises all day long, and then sent to bed at 9:00 p.m. But even after the lights went out, the work continued — there were dirty rifles to clean and toilets to scrub. (We used to joke that we were expected to be "An Officer and a Janitor." But our real-life version of the movie definitely wasn't a love story.) Some lucky candidates even got to stand in a two-hour "fire watch" shift between lights out and reveille to ensure that all the weapons locked up in the squad bay were guarded.

And then, of course, we'd wake up at 5:00 the next morning to do it all over again.

By week three, the midpoint of the training, I was so sleep-deprived that minor tasks that should have been easy, like re-calling some of the lessons I'd been learning or even just lacing up my boots, seemed extremely difficult. And when I was in the middle of this fog, it was tough to see the meaning behind it. I now know that the early stages of military training are designed to test future officers to see how well they perform when they're both exhausted and stressed. After all, we really do behave differently when we're maxed out — and my behavior under stress was exactly what the Corps wanted to assess.

It's these moments that reveal whether you can be counted on to do the right thing when tested. Can you uphold the Corps' character standards when you've got little left to give? Can you be trusted? When you're starving and tired and there's only one prepacked meal left, do you take it for yourself? Or do you share it with the team? When you've lost your belt buckle and can't find it before the inspection, do you own up to your mistake — or do you panic and grab someone else's to make sure your uniform is complete? What superficially seems like haphazard chaos to be endured is actually one giant lab experiment in character development and assessment. If you can't do the right things in a training environment, the Corps has no interest in seeing whether you can do the right thing in combat — there's just too much at stake.

If you were able to look at my "grades" during training to see how I was performing, you might have thought I was failing. If this had been a reality TV series and I had a camera on me 24/7, I would've looked like a hot mess. I was yelled at for having a messy gear locker and called on the carpet for my inability to remember various Marine Corps facts and figures. I also stumbled many times on the parade ground while marching around. I even dropped my rifle on several occasions — a cardinal sin in the Corps. So each week, as I watched other candidates either drop out or be asked to leave, I thought it was just a matter of time until my number came up. Fortunately, it never did.

It was only after my OCS experience that I realized why I passed. The Corps wasn't looking for tactical perfection. The sergeant instructors who lead candidates through OCS recognize that they are working with imperfect students who are eager to learn; they also realize the stressful nature of the environment they create. After all, they created it! Since the candidates are so caught up in the training, what they don't notice is that during the early stages of training there's an acceptance of less-than-best performance at the hundreds of tasks you must complete each day — that is, *as long as you don't compromise your character.* That's a big caveat.

To assist candidates in doing the right thing in moments of stress, we were told to always abide by the Corps' values of honor, courage, and commitment. If we could demonstrate these three behaviors when challenged, we were told, we would be welcomed into the organization.

Through the experience of having the concept of values literally spelled out for me and reinforced by strong examples, I now realize how easy (relatively speaking) my Marine Corps character development process was compared to what happens with my peers in the private sector. The truth is, most professionals don't get the opportunity to explore, validate, align, or test their values in a controlled environment. Having no such opportunities can prevent them from becoming Sparks who can rely on themselves to do the right thing — or at least right by themselves — when challenged. Doing the right thing is the foundation on which trust is built.

WHY YOUR VALUES MATTER

When most people embark on their careers, the onboarding process provided by their new employer is fairly straightforward: "Here's your desk, here's the HR manual, do this . . . don't do that . . . and here are your colleagues. Get to work." Before they know it, they're off to the races without much thought about values, either theirs or the organization's.

Organizational values are important, and if you work at a company that has them, as we did when we were in the military, great. It's nice to know that someone at the top has thought about the qualities that employees should aspire to have. But on your Spark journey, don't start by thinking about your organization's values first — you can work on those later. Start by thinking about your *own* values.

Your values are the principles or qualities that are important to you — like fairness, family, humor, freedom, justice, humility, faith, or adventure. Your values are deeply personal, and whether you know it or not, you've been developing them your whole life. They've been inspired by your family, your religion, or powerful experiences, like the loss of a parent, the birth of a child, or a significant and hard-earned accomplishment. Values also evolve over time — what you valued as a teen may be very different from what you value as an adult.

When your values are active in your life, they can serve many purposes, from providing the hard line you don't cross (*I'm not going to engage in this accounting practice because I think it's misleading*) to showing you the way forward (*I'm not going to have different standards for our team — I don't think it's fair*). Values can serve as your North Star, guiding you when you're making some of life's important decisions (*Should I take over the family business? Should I shift industries at this stage in my career?*). Sometimes a quick consultation with your values can lead you to a good choice. When you make difficult choices that align with your values, you'll always find yourself sleeping better at night. On the other hand, when you make decisions without regard to your values, you can wind up asking yourself: *Why doesn't this choice feel right?* Many poor choices can be avoided if we think first about our values before taking action.

This became apparent to one of our colleagues, who had spent the better part of her professional life developing her expertise on health care reform. At one point in her career she was working for a small, private consultancy doing policy work with a great group of people. So when she got a phone call about an opportunity to work for a much larger firm — one she described as the "place where all policy wonks want to live, work, and die" — she was torn. *Should I stay here with this awesome team,* she asked herself, *or go work at this ah-mazing organization?* At the time she couldn't resist adding this experience to her résumé, so she made the difficult decision to leave her role and pursue the new position.

When she arrived, there was immediate culture shock. She was used to cordial colleagues who would stop in the hallways and engage in conversations about work, life, and everything in between. But not at her new job. Everyone seemed so serious and stiff. *This must be why they're so successful — there's no time for small talk,* she reasoned, and so she kept her head down to focus solely on work.

Several months into her new role, she experienced a significant life event that made her question her recent career decision: she was in a serious car crash that left her bedridden for nearly three weeks. During her recovery she received a card and a check-in call from her employer, but overall the support she experienced was impersonal; she was left feeling lonely and with a deep sense that she had made the wrong decision to leave her former team. While she felt that her intellectual contributions mattered to her employer, she just didn't feel that *she* did.

During this time she realized that prestige wasn't as important to her as relationships. She not only wanted but *valued* working with engaged colleagues who cared about her. It didn't take her long to call her former manager and beg for her old role back. Fortunately, it didn't take much begging. They welcomed her back with open arms. Not only did the firm regain a committed and loyal employee (a Spark!), but our colleague arrived at her old job with a renewed sense of her values and confidence in what really mattered most to her.

Making choices that are aligned with our most deeply held values can be validating, both personally and professionally. These decisions free you, mentally speaking, to live up to your Spark potential because you're not distracted by what's going wrong with your life and trying to fix it. Instead, you're focused on leveraging and capitalizing on what is actually going right. There's something internally gratifying about knowing that the precious moments of our lives are directed toward satisfying pursuits rather than energy-wasting endeavors. This is the sweet spot that every Spark wants to find — the place where we have access to the *flow* experience, that positive energy we feel when we're deeply engrossed in our passions and able to channel our efforts into something meaningful and results-oriented.

But that doesn't mean it's easy to make decisions that complement our values. The difficulty comes from the trade-offs that are necessary to achieve alignment. Sometimes those trade-offs are small (*I can no longer watch* Keeping Up with the Kardashians *after that episode ... I'm going to start setting my alarm earlier so I can get ahead of the day*), but sometimes they can be substantial. You might have to give up something you find very gratifying to gain something that you value even more. Any type of change can also require a lot of emotional energy and discomfort as you adapt to your choices.

But the results of your efforts to align your values with your decisions are more than worth it, because through these choices you honor your future self — that person you aspire to be twenty, thirty, or forty years from now. Your tough choices will add up to a life your future self will be proud to have lived. No one wants to look back and regret what they didn't do in critical moments. Living your values is the best way to prevent this from ever happening.

THE VALUES CONNECTION

Sean's Story

I shared earlier that I made some pretty significant decisions in my life that led to finding myself in the Air Force. The Air Force afforded me the opportunity to become a leader. And in the earliest seasons of my career, I thought that the Air Force would be my professional home forever. But a lot happened between the time I joined and the time I left: unbeknownst to me at first, as I was growing personally and professionally, my values and priorities were shifting.

For starters, I got married, which certainly affected my values. When my wife Vera and I were newlyweds, personal independence and risk became less important to me and family and security became a top priority. This didn't happen overnight — it was more like an evolution. And I probably wouldn't have even been able to articulate this change until my son Connor was born. His arrival quickly pulled this values transition into focus.

There are few words to describe the feeling of holding your child for the very first time. What I vividly remember is being overwhelmed by a sense of responsibility. I wanted Connor's experience as a child to be different from mine. My parents divorced when I was young; though they did the very best they could to raise their four sons, after the divorce the arrangement wasn't optimal. My youngest two brothers lived with my mom, and the second oldest and I lived with my dad. While we certainly saw each other, there were many times when I wished that we could all just be together. As I looked at my newborn son and realized there was a chance I could miss out on half of his childhood because of all the deployments on my horizon, I knew I had to start thinking about making some difficult choices. The only way I could be more present was to rethink my service in the Air Force. To become the father I wanted to be, I might have to give up something I loved doing.

After thinking long and hard about my options, I started with a compromise. I transitioned out of the Air Force and accepted a role with the Air National Guard in Montgomery, Alabama, reasoning that even though I wouldn't be flying and serving full-time, I'd still be flying and serving. And better yet, my family and I could spend more time together. In theory, this was the best fit for everyone and a great idea . . . until we arrived in Montgomery.

The region just didn't work for Connor. The allergens present in the local environment made him very sick. So sick he was hospitalized two times in the first year of his life because he needed help breathing. He even spent his first Christmas in the hospital. For any parent who is reading this, you know what it's like to see your child suffering — not only did I feel helpless, but I felt responsible. I had done this to him by moving to a new environment. Now, rationally, I know this wasn't true — but it certainly felt true at the time.

This was when I knew that even more difficult choices needed to be made. Vera and I recognized that despite our affinity for our new squadron and the region, we just couldn't live there long-term. Our physician recommended that we move closer to the coast, which he felt would help Connor's respiratory challenges. Even though Vera and I had just moved and certainly weren't looking forward to another move, we saw this as an opportunity to further live our values of family. We decided to move to Bradenton, Florida, to be closer to her parents and to my mom.

As for me and my career, suddenly I was at a crossroads. *What am I going to do now?* I wondered. One thing was clear: I wouldn't be flying F-16s anymore. There were no more reserve squadrons I could transfer to, and I had already made the decision not to pursue an active-duty role. My time as a military officer was coming to a close. I had no choice but to swallow this bitter pill.

I can still remember my final F-16 flight and the last time I stepped out of the cockpit and walked across the tarmac toward the hangar. (I may have looked back a few times, and I will neither confirm nor deny whether there were tears in my eyes.) I knew I was saying good-bye to a dream that had meant so much to me. But in those moments I found resolve because deep down I knew I was making the right decision.

I was lucky too. In my transition process, I was hired by Delta Airlines, which meant that I didn't have to give up flying altogether. I was assigned to the 737. While flying the 737 wasn't as much fun as a fighter jet, I still was flying and still felt connected to my military service, since many Delta pilots were Veterans like me.

I also felt at peace with my choice because I was living my values. I now know that understanding your values and living them is the best insurance policy you can get in life — and all it costs is reflection, commitment, and fortitude. Living your values prevents you from making choices you'll regret, or even muttering the phrase "If only I had . . ." later in life, because you feel that you did everything you could to fulfill the expectations you had for yourself. From where I sit today, I have zero regrets . . . and a ton of amazing memories of watching Connor growing up.

YOUR VALUES: DEVELOPING POSITIVE SELF-FULFILLING PROPHECIES

One of the most important leadership lessons we share with Sparks is that before you lead others, you have to be able to lead yourself. Self-leadership requires that you give yourself direction. It's creating a pathway where there's no paved road. So, for instance, if you want a promotion, self-leadership is seeking to understand what stakeholders are looking for in an ideal candidate for promotion and developing yourself accordingly and in ways consistent with your leadership style. Your values can serve as an internal compass, giving you a sense of where it is you actually want to go. Being aware of your values can even serve as a positive self-fulfilling prophecy.

The Galatea Effect — which has been researched in a variety of scenarios and whose name refers to a Greek myth about an ivory statue that comes to life — suggests that our images, beliefs, and ideas about ourselves have a powerful influence on our behavior. For instance, if you know you value honesty, you'll be the person who speaks truth even when it's uncomfortable to do so. Or if you know you value dependability, you won't blow off a volunteering obligation on a Saturday even though you'd rather sleep in. In the workplace, your values can be reflected in your performance. If you know you value excellence, it'll show up in the work products you produce. If you value teamwork, you'll work with others collaboratively to drive results. These values are all, of course, the hallmarks of a Spark. The more you believe in your values, the more you will become them. That's the Galatea Effect.

But if you're not sure of what you value, you're in a vulnerable place. When you're disconnected from your priorities in life, your self-identity is up for grabs and you lose the opportunity to lead your life in a positive manner. Instead, your life is leading you. The direction that it's heading in might be good . . . *but it also might be not as good as it could be.* When you get to the destination your life has been leading you toward, it might feel incredibly unfulfilling and frustrating as you realize you are not the Spark you want to be.

It could be that deep down inside you value family but the choices you've made without regard to that value have allowed your digital life to take precedence over being present for your family. Now you miss out on opportunities to really connect with others. Or perhaps somewhere deep inside you truly value your physical health, but your lack of focus on physical fitness or healthy eating has led you to a place where the simplest exercises are more difficult than you'd like them to be.

You might not even be aware that there's a disconnect between your actions and your values. It's not like a disconnect happens overnight. But one choice can gradually lead to another, and incrementally you may find that the way you live your life is at odds with your intentions. Not only can this lead to serious disappointment, but it can also lead you to a place where you lose influence with others because the disconnect in your life is equally obvious to them. This chips away at their trust in you.

Simply put, others just may not believe you are who you say you are, or that, under pressure, you'll act like you say you'll act. Why? Because they've observed the little inconsistencies in how you live your life. Like the manager who says he values work-life balance but constantly emails you throughout the weekend. Or the colleague who says she values collaboration but hoards all the work so she can take the credit for it. Or the clients who say they value candor but get very defensive when given any kind of feedback. All these disconnects create roadblocks for people who are trying to trust one another.

Of course, we're all really good (and quick!) at pointing out how our values differ from other people's values. But that's not as important as our ability to point out the values disconnect *within ourselves*. Acknowledging the internal disconnect between values and actions is where true growth takes place.

DEVELOPING YOUR INNER VALUES

To avoid the disconnect between your values and actions, be a Spark who takes personal character development seriously. You can do this by determining which key values are most important to you. This type of work is best done in a quiet place, which is often difficult to find in this day and age. But when done well, this internal work can force you to confront some hard truths in your life.

Disconnecting yourself for a few hours from work so you can think seriously and deeply about what matters most to you is hard to do and a serious challenge. In the working world today we emphasize doing, not thinking. We're all constantly busy, moving so fast that it's hard to find the time to slow down. But failure to do so could result in missed opportunities to make choices to become the Spark you want to be. So invest the time in seeking to uncover your values, and you'll be led to discover any misalignment between your expectations of yourself and your actions.

The next step is having an honest conversation with yourself so that you not only understand where, when, and why you've compromised your values in the past but also recognize the changes you need to make to lead more consistently with your intentions. Then prepare to get uncomfortable. Change is hard! Change doesn't come without some pain, whether it's physical, like grueling through a new workout routine, or mental, like convincing yourself to stand up for your point of view in meetings. But once you start working through your discomfort, you will appreciate and embrace the discipline you've been building to become the person you want to be.

An important note: In your journey it's important to reflect on who you can enlist to support you. This point is key. Sparks recognize that no one achieves lasting success on their own. As humans, we crave community. We all want — and can benefit greatly from — connections with people who encourage us to be our best and help us confront our blind spots. Plus, there are limits to any one person's ability to reason, think bigger, persevere, and demonstrate grace. We need other Sparks around to leverage their collective intelligence and wisdom and apply it in our lives.

THE ENODIA SOCIETY

Courtney's Story

I've naturally sought connections with people, and I love hanging out in groups. Throughout my life I've enjoyed being a part of some pretty cool ones. Whether it was my "Fab Five Friends" in high school, my sorority sisters at North Carolina State University, or the "fraternity" I joined when I became a Marine, I've always gravitated toward groups of people. Even when it comes to exercise.

Angie has this theory related to running: there are dog people, and there are cat people. The dog people are social runners who enjoy the company of others, whereas the cat people just want to do their own thing. Well, Angie is definitely a cat person . . . and I'm definitely a dog person. I just don't get cats . . . who wants to run, bike, or swim alone? Besides, my best workouts come when I'm with the pack. I like being pushed by others — I find this is when I perform at my best.

The same goes for my professional life. I seek out others who challenge me intellectually, share their wisdom freely, and hold me accountable to my goals. I've also found that a sound group of advisers keeps me sharp and ensures that my values and actions remain congruent.

I've been fortunate throughout my career to encounter so many professionals with whom I could share strong connections and this type of mutual candor. But I didn't think about it all that much until my midthirties, when my friend Andrea approached me with the idea of routinely engaging with other like-minded women to become more purposeful with our development. "It'll be like a mastermind group, Courtney," she said, and right away I was interested. She described the group as a place where we could create and pursue the goals that mattered most to us while receiving honest, compassionate feedback and support. When she mentioned the other women who were considering membership, I was convinced that being a part of this talented group would be a worthwhile experience. I was in.

Andrea, Helen, Carolyn, Marsha, and I came together to form the Enodia Society. The word "Enodia" refers to reinvention and development beyond challenges and crossroads. Through the years we've become sounding boards, accountability partners, idea generators, and fierce supporters of each other's professional and personal development.

Our format is simple. We connect monthly for a ninety-minute call. During each call one of us is "up," meaning it's that member's turn to submit her goals, progress, and challenges to the group. That person typically sends her thoughts in writing to the group prior to the call when she's up. Then, during the group conference call, after we catch up personally, the member being featured that month reviews her report and asks the group for guidance on specific matters. The topics we share our perspectives on are wide-ranging, covering our careers, lives, families, and dreams. Enodia members never disappoint in their candor and commitment. In the many years we've been conducting calls, we've had only one call in which someone was unable to participate.

These calls have been incredibly challenging for me, as my fellow members don't hold back on their feedback. I remember one time when I expressed concern about Lead Star's strategy. I had prepared an overview of where the business was going, who our ideal clients were, and what our plans were for expanding. My fellow Enodia members celebrated my success, but then held my feet to the fire on those parts of the strategy they thought were unrealistic. They also shared best practices they thought I could use to revise the plan and expand our business development efforts. Prior to the call, I had hoped they would endorse my plan wholeheartedly, though knowing they knew my values and goals made me respect their feedback and take it all to heart because I knew they were looking out for me.

It's great to have these four amazing women in my corner as we experience life together. Being able to reflect on my successes and failures has been clarifying and has allowed me to calibrate my actions against my values at critical times in my life. I appreciate the trust we've built by consistently showing up honestly for each other. The Enodia Society really has made my success possible by keeping me accountable to becoming better, and there's no greater joy than celebrating success with them. There's also no greater comfort than knowing that when I start to drift away from my values, the Enodia ladies will let me know and help get me back on track.

WHEN WE COMPROMISE OUR VALUES

As you become more familiar with your values on your Spark journey and work to make them more active in your life, it's important to bear in mind that the real world doesn't always congratulate you and embrace your self-development pursuits. In fact, sometimes it seems like the real world is plotting against you and undermining your efforts to be a Spark. It's best to be prepared for these situations so that you know how to manage them or even avoid them altogether.

It's important to know, for instance, that it's when we're busy that we're most vulnerable to compromising our values. In a famous study, groups of theology students, after rehearsing the story of the Good Samaritan, were told to walk across campus to a classroom where they could be filmed preaching the sermon.* Along the way, each study group encountered a man who was clearly distressed and in need. Just about all of the students who weren't under any kind of time pressure to walk across campus stopped to help the man out. But when the students were released late from class and felt some pressure to hurry to the room where they'd be filmed, only 63 percent stopped to help the man. And when students were directly told to hurry to get to the other classroom, only 10 percent stopped to offer support.

The lesson here is simple: if theologians, who are poised to do good and primed with the Good Samaritan message, can find themselves behaving in ways inconsistent with their own expectations of themselves, it's safe to say that we're all equally at risk. Holding true to our values is challenging for all of us.

In addition to the time factor, we're also more likely to compromise our values — *and even our ethics* — when we're tired and stressed. As our working day wears on and we become more physiologically depleted because we used up most of our focus and energy in the morning, we have less willpower in the afternoon to do the right thing. When we're tired and stressed,

---

* John M. Darley and C. Daniel Batson, "'From Jerusalem to Jericho': A Study of Situational and Dispositional Variables in Helping Behavior," *Journal of Personality and Social Psychology* 27, no. 1 (July 1973): 100–108.

not only are we less likely to enact our values, but we're more tempted to lie, cheat, or steal.

Researchers have referred to this as the Morning Morality Effect: we're better positioned to act ethically earlier in the day than later on.* Maryam Kouchaki, a researcher at Harvard University, has conducted several studies on this effect and concluded that her subjects were 20 to 50 percent more likely to be dishonest in the afternoon than in the morning. She also found that the effect is difficult to avoid regardless of where you are on the ethical scale. We're all susceptible to unethical behavior.

So what's a Spark supposed to do? Who's not rushed, tired, or stressed at some point during the day? Our best advice is to develop strategies for yourself by slowing down and giving yourself a few breaks in the day so you don't reach your melting point. Rather than eating lunch at your desk, get some fresh air and eat outside so you can reset your energy for the afternoon. Schedule critical meetings in the morning, when you have greater energy to make tough decisions. Look at your calendar weeks in advance and block out thirty-minute breaks in your mornings and afternoons to protect your ability to take time to recharge your batteries.

This type of self-management is essential not just for living out your values but also for ensuring that your performance is high. And again, consult your values frequently so that you have a ready reference for how you want to behave when tested. We've even met professionals who printed out their values and posted them near their computer so they would have a reminder

---

* Maryam Kouchaki and Isaac H. Smith, "The Morning Morality Effect: The Influence of Time of Day on Unethical Behavior," *Psychological Science* 25, no. 1 (2014): 95–102.

— front and center — whenever they felt challenged and needed inspiration.

THE GATEWAY TO LEADERSHIP

Leading with your own values is the gateway to leading others. If you know who you are and what you stand for, you're able to sit up straighter and be more self-assured. You begin to develop self-trust because you know how you'll behave when challenged and know that you'll be able to count on yourself when the chips are down. And if you can count on yourself, there's no doubt that others can count on you too.

People who live their values exude a quiet confidence — they worry less about what others think and instead focus on being true to themselves. That shows up as an authenticity that's refreshing to others. We grant followership to those people in our organizations we perceive as authentic — that is, the people who aren't playing politics, who aren't always trying to say the "right things" to whomever they're talking to, who aren't seeking popularity in exchange for their integrity.

And if you're able to convey to others that it's okay to be real, you can have a definite impact in your organization.

We've seen this effect among many of the emerging leaders we've mentored — those professionals who were tapped for greater responsibility in their organizations but had never really received leadership training. One was an associate who came to us with questions on how to fit in. He felt that as he grew in the organization, he needed to change in order to become more like the senior managers he observed. We challenged him by asking, "What do you think exactly you need to change? Your organization thinks you're great, which is why you're getting leadership training so you can be even better."

He then confessed that he felt insecure about acting like himself because he was so different from his managers. "I don't have a lot in common with them," he shared. "I really think I need a major overhaul on how I behave at work." After advising him that any type of major life reconstruction would not only undermine but also derail his efforts, we then spent time helping him understand his values and how they could be manifested in an authentic leadership style that would be right for him. His leadership style would also be grounded in other Spark behaviors that would ensure his credibility with others.

We heard back from him several months later with some great news. "We've been hiring a lot of new associates, and I can't begin to tell you how many associates have sought me out because they felt like I was someone they could talk to — because they saw themselves in me. You have no idea how affirming this is to me! It makes me feel like I'm truly making a difference at work."

And we can't think of anything more validating and rewarding than being a Spark whose personal example can positively influence and inspire in a way that adds value to others.

SPARK ACTIONS

To be a Spark, you've got to do the tough work on yourself first. Follow these steps to begin understanding and expressing your values:

- Find a quiet place and dedicate time to reflecting on the values that are most important to you. Identify a list of your top five most important values.
- Assess your support network — the people you can rely on as you develop your Spark behaviors. Work to ensure that these people stay present in your life.

- Understand the circumstances in which you have tended to compromise your values. Work to manage your schedule so as to avoid these situations.

CHARGING AHEAD

Your Spark development happens when you work on keeping your values present in your life as well as developing strategies that allow you to live up to your expectations of yourself. The following resources are available on www.sparkslead.us to help you bring your actions into alignment with your values:

- *Character:* Have you ever identified your top values? This exercise will lead you through a values identification process and help you explore how you can make your values more active in your life. We also offer you a leader's guide to help you lead this exercise for your team.
- *Mentors:* Have you ever wondered about the people in your corner — who they are, how they help you, and what you can glean from their experiences? This exercise allows you to reflect on and identify your mentors (or prospective mentors). We also give you guidance on how to approach mentors to ask for their insight and guidance.

Once you're finished, you'll be ready to jump right into chapter 3, which is focused on sharpening your performance so that others will view you as a credible Spark who brings excellence to everything that you do.

3

THE FOUR KEYS TO
BEING CREDIBLE

Credibility is the foundation of your leadership style. It allows people to view you as dependable, trustworthy, and committed. Sparks who demonstrate the four keys to credibility can quickly generate trust among others.

M ANY OF US PLOW through the day without giving much thought to the impact we have on others. Most of us are balancing schedules, managing tasks, responding to customers, and juggling priorities. It's easy to get tunnel vision while whittling away at our daily to-do lists and lose awareness of how we are actively engaging with others.

The problem is that this lack of awareness can be detrimental: too often we either miss out on opportunities to be a Spark in our environment or accidentally behave in ways that undermine the influence we're trying to build with the key people around us. That's what happens when you schedule back-to-back meetings on Thursday, leaving no margin for error, and your 2:00 p.m. runs long. You rush into your next meeting delivering an apology ("I'm so sorry, my other meeting ran over") to a frustrated group. Or maybe your lack of awareness of your impact on others is affecting your personal life. Do you tell your friends, "I promise we'll get together soon — I'll call you!" but then never reach out to them, despite your best intentions? Have you noticed that they're starting to lose faith in you?

You may be genuinely sorry you're inconveniencing others and don't mean to make empty promises, but there is a price to pay when you don't follow through on your commitments: your credibility suffers. Over time you'll go from being the dependable, go-to person to someone who is viewed as unreliable and delivers inconsistent results. It's difficult to lead change, or to jump-start a team project, when others are skeptical about relying on you.

Credibility is a critical Spark quality because it contributes to the trust people place in you. And one of the most challenging aspects of credibility is that you really can't force people to trust you — you have to earn their trust in ways that are meaningful to them (not you). Credibility is solely in the eye of the beholder, and you have to work hard to understand what makes you credible to others so that you know the criteria that you're being evaluated against.

Fortunately, there is a recipe for credibility. It's the combination of your character and your performance level. To be a Spark, you can't have one without the other. You can't be a person of sound integrity but a low performer and expect to have influence with others. Likewise, if you're getting results but achieving them in inconsistent and sometimes underhanded ways, you're never going to build trust.

We just talked about character in chapter 2. Let's turn our attention to the action steps you can take to keep your performance level high so that others will recognize you as a Spark who leads in thought, word, and deed.

INTRODUCING THE FOUR KEY ACTIONS
THAT CREDIBLE SPARKS NEED TO TAKE

Every organization wants high performers, but many can't quite pinpoint what qualities define them. So they look to numerical outcomes, like sales quotas, outputs, and other easy-to-measure criteria that often show up on employee evaluations: "Lisa closed twenty loans last month — the highest in the district," or "Peter processed 10 percent more claims than anyone else in the region last quarter," or "Tamara's crew achieved 95 percent efficiency on the production line last night."

To be a Spark, you need to influence outcomes. But your credibility isn't going to be earned just by the end game stats. It will be the *manner* in which you achieve your results that determines if you're truly credible to others (or not). So if you're working with others to achieve success, it's important that every interaction with you is reassuring to them.

This can be demonstrated by implementing the four keys to credibility that ensure a high level of performance:

- Understanding and meeting the standards of others
- Having a very narrow "say-do gap"
- Communicating your intent and expectations to others
- Holding others accountable when they fail to meet standards

These four actions are interdependent, and each can be undertaken with conscious effort. But the challenge is that they become progressively more difficult as each new action is introduced.

UNDERSTANDING AND MEETING THE STANDARDS OF OTHERS

Courtney's Story

To be a Spark, you have to meet standards, whether they are your organization's standards or the standards of the people you work with. This is the important first step toward having influence over others. If you can't do the easy things that are bright-lined in your job description, found on your employee evaluation, or communicated directly to you by either a manager or a peer, it'll be nearly impossible for you to be credible. Beyond the obvious, like showing up on time, it's the little things that build credibility, like meeting deadlines, being responsive, demonstrating quality in work products, and being approachable.

But there are also the *unspoken* expectations that others have of you. These may not always be clear but are critically important. On your Spark journey, you need to be curious about discovering what these often unstated or understated standards are so that you know not only what you're being measured against but what you can do to take your already good performance to a whole new level — a Spark level. Discerning and then rising to these standards will allow you to be a true standout in your organization and will earn you the influence necessary to lead people to exceptional results.

The Marine Corps did a very good job of teeing me up for this type of investigative work. The organization had a ton of standards they were measuring my performance against, like procedural knowledge and physical fitness. But my training instructors also prepared me for my very first managerial role by sharing that beyond the Corps' expectations, my Marines would have certain expectations of me — though they wouldn't be forthcoming in telling me what they were.

In other words, when I reported to my first duty station, I wasn't going to be met by a corporal with a binder saying, "Here, ma'am. To lead us effectively, you can read and digest these tips and ideas I've written up for you." It was on me to figure out what success would look like in all my relationships and to gain a very clear picture of what I needed to do to be a strong performer.

So one of the very first things I did when I was stationed in Okinawa, Japan, was to get to know my Marines — and their families — very well. I wanted to create a true sense of candor so I could initiate dialogues about what my team expected of me and so that they too felt comfortable approaching me with their expectations. I knew my efforts had paid off when a Marine's wife approached me and said that she wished I could do a better job of planning family events so that everyone could get to know each other better. Not only was her insight helpful, but it gave me insight into how others were evaluating my performance. Once I understood their expectations, I took it as a personal responsibility to meet them. When I did, I discovered that the level of trust and cooperation among my team increased because we all were looking out for one another.

What I've observed over time is that many professionals, even the most conscientious of the bunch, don't spend enough time considering the perspectives of key stakeholders. It's not that they don't care or think that alternative perspectives are unimportant; rather, they either assume they're doing what they need to be doing or don't know how to go about uncovering information about other perspectives.

Let's start with assumptions. Too often we fail to examine our behavior at work because we fall into routines. We naturally think that our way of performing our work is the right way because, after all, we've always done it that way and no one has told us anything different. But this approach leaves many opportunities to build influence on the table. This was clear in a recent project we performed for the American Society for Radiation Oncology (ASTRO).

When we were asked by ASTRO to develop a training program for its physician members, our goal was to help physicians develop their leadership skills so they could have greater influence in leading their teams through the industry's transformation. When conducting research for the program, we visited various hospitals and clinics throughout the country to interview physicians and key stakeholders — nurses, patients, billing staff, and other department physicians — and gain as complete a picture as possible of what successful physicians do to demonstrate high performance and earn credibility in all their relationships. Their answers to our questions were exhaustive and very diverse and went far beyond the technical competencies of the role. In the end, the results of our research were pretty surprising.

Nurses shared that the best physicians were knowledgeable, respectful, and accountable for mistakes. Patients wanted physicians to have compassion and a calming bedside manner. Patients' families wanted doctors to give them information in ways that made sense to them. Billing staff wanted physicians to understand how to fill out charts completely so that they could bill accurately. Other physicians wanted their colleagues to demonstrate expertise and get published, and residents wanted mentoring. It seemed as if everyone in the world of radiation oncologists wanted them to become credible leaders. When we shared our results with ASTRO members, one blurted out, "I went to school for nearly ten years, and no one ever talked about how to become a leader. I think we all just assumed we were leaders. I wish I had known this when I started out in my practice."

In this physician's defense, we often become so focused on the technical and tactical aspects of training when we're learning our job that we can easily overlook the "people" aspect of our role. Then we build routines, assuming that we're doing right by all the parties we engage with. It's often not that we're harming our relationships, but that, with a little more knowledge and a little more discipline in adjusting our interactions with others, we could be doing much, much better.

After we delivered the ASTRO leadership training program, I stayed in contact with many of the physician participants. Those who modified their behaviors to meet the expectations of key stakeholders shared that their relationships with their team members improved in many productive — and sometimes economically advantageous — ways.

I challenge you to start uncovering these unspoken standards by paying attention to your environment and inferring what your stakeholders value. Also observe your organization's most successful employees and ascertain what standards they're meeting that make them so influential.

I once asked a coaching client to do just this. My client was intelligent and well educated, and she did exceptional work for her firm. Her challenge was that she wasn't getting picked for higher-visibility assignments. She learned through observation that those who did get the plum projects took the time to network internally by inviting senior leaders out to coffee and volunteering for projects (as opposed to just waiting around for someone to ask them to join a new team). Once she realized that these types of behaviors were among the unstated expectations that, if met, would be rewarded, she developed the courage to demonstrate them too.

Another important consideration as you discover the critical standards in your environment is that even if meeting some of these expectations feels uncomfortable to you or they don't quite mesh with what you want to be doing, they remain important to others. To cultivate influence, you can't adopt a cafeteria-style approach to meeting standards; you can't say, *I like this one, I'll take it,* or, *I don't like this one, so I'm going to ignore it.* This approach will quickly make you an inconsistent performer.

So while you might hate filing your expense report at the end of the week, or don't want to wear your safety goggles while touring the plant, remember that your preferences don't matter. To be a Spark, you must not only know what's expected of you but always perform to the level of excellence that you would demand from yourself (and others) against all the standards that have been set for you.

Understanding and meeting the standards of others is the first level of achieving high performance. The next level also relates to standards — not the ones coming from your organization or from other people, but the ones that you yourself communicate.

NARROWING YOUR SAY-DO GAP

The "say-do gap" is the space between your words and your actions. When it's small, you're consistent. When it's large, you're at risk of frustrating others. You may know this already because you've probably been on the receiving end of some people with a large say-do gap.

Imagine you're working with a vendor who assures you, "You'll get this project by the fifteenth." You say to yourself, *Excellent. That works well.* And then on the thirteenth the vendor sends you an email saying, "Remember that deadline? We need to push it a week." You think, *Um, okay.* Then, when the new deadline pops up, the work product arrives at the close of the day and what you receive doesn't even come close to what the vendor promised to deliver.

What just happened? The vendor compromised its say-do gap by not following through with the expectations it set at the get-go. What do you do? Chances are you'll be pretty hesitant to work with this vendor again. It lost credibility in your eyes and its performance level just doesn't make the cut.

Just as organizations have say-do gaps, people have them too. Knowing this, Sparks always ensure that they honor every commitment they make throughout the day by following through, because they know what's at risk if they let their standards slide — their influence. You earn influence when you demonstrate a consistently high level of performance. And your say-do gap is a great gauge for monitoring your performance because it keeps you honest about how well you're living up to the expectations you have set.

Developing this level of consistency is tough to do because you have to set expectations that you're 100 percent certain you can follow through on. What happens when you say at a meeting, "I'll get this project done for you by Friday," and then you get back to your desk and realize that you forgot about an all-day client meeting on Thursday? That's going to make it difficult to turn the project around by Friday, but a Spark wouldn't go back and try to reset expectations; instead, if you're a Spark, you make a Herculean effort to follow through on your commitment because your reputation is at stake. Your commitments are critical, and not honoring them should be a true exception to the rule, not the norm.

Sometimes it's difficult to uphold high standards in a workplace where everyone else is comfortable with less-than-best expectations. It's true that in some work environments people become complacent about standards — they arrive to work whenever, they show up late for meetings, and they are too accepting of excuses for poor performance. As a Spark, you may find it difficult to step up and model a narrow say-do gap when no one else seems to notice or care.

But leadership isn't what you expect from others, but what

you demonstrate to those around you. And what we've seen is that if you're just one Spark modeling high performance and paying attention to your say-do gap, others will be inspired by you and be quick to follow you.

We saw this when we worked with Facebook prior to its initial public offering (IPO). Many professionals were moving at the speed of light to help the organization scale. One of our clients expressed concern over the pace of the quick transactions. She didn't want to get sloppy and damage relationships with ad agencies if they couldn't deliver what they promised. To try to prevent this outcome, she adopted the say-do gap principle for herself and encouraged others to do the same. What she observed was that as soon as her team members had set up strict language around personal credibility, her team was able to cultivate a team identity around delivering high performance. And as we shared earlier, organizations that are credible deliver meaningful results.

Because you, like our client, are most likely not going to achieve the results you seek by yourself, the next aspect of high performance is ensuring that the teams you're a part of are focused on success.

COMMUNICATING YOUR INTENT AND EXPECTATIONS TO OTHERS

As more organizations use matrices to manage their teams, many professionals find themselves reporting to multiple bosses, serving on several teams, and using the terms "straight line," "dotted line," or "indirect report" when referring to their work ecosystem. Added to the mix are the many virtual relationships that most professionals have to support, as well as client or vendor relationships to manage. All in all, today's professionals are engaged with a workforce that is increasingly diverse along gender, cultural, ethnic, and generational lines.

All of these dynamics can sometimes generate confusion and uncertainty around achieving success through other people. In these increasingly common types of environments, Sparks often emerge from the pack by taking the initiative to bring clarity and focus to their teams. They do so by communicating intent and expectations.

The idea of "intent" is interesting. The three of us first learned about it and used it professionally when we were in the military. The idea was that when we were leading teams in combat, someone located far away from us was calling the shots. The commander would decide what the unit was going to do and share it with the next line of reports, who would transmit the commander's order down several levels until it got to us. It may seem surprising that, unlike what happens in the childhood game of "Telephone," the order wasn't compromised by the time we received it. What allowed the order to stick was the notion of the commander's "intent."

At every level of communication, the big boss's intentions — what he or she wanted to happen — were passed along. But we were never instructed in *how* to achieve the result. That was on us to figure out because, unlike the commander, we were present at the point of action. And since we were often separated by distance and unable to communicate with the person driving the action, that person relied on us to perform in a way consistent with expectations. We always knew what to do, and even if the situation on the ground was changing, our objective wasn't. This gave us a lot of room to take initiative without losing sight of the goal.

Having this level of initiative was incredibly freeing because it inspired creative problem-solving, which is not only highly prized in the military but always on demand in the private sector.

In fact, we often get calls from managers who wish that their teams were better able to take initiative to solve problems rather than bumping them up to management — like working to solve their own IT issues, coordinating meeting space for the team conference, or handling disputes with colleagues. We've worked with these managers to help them understand how to communicate more clearly in order to create the conditions for initiative to happen. This sometimes requires that managers dial down their efforts to control their teams by telling them what to do and how to do it. While commanding creates compliance, it also drives low performance because team members don't feel valued or empowered. From there it's a slippery slope to disengagement.

We always encourage managers to share the "what" that needs to happen and then leave the "how" up to team members. Interestingly, when managers back off from their need to control, they're quickly surprised by how creative and successful their teams can be without their direct involvement.

You don't need to be a manager to create the conditions for initiative to happen. All you need to do when working with your colleagues is share your vision for success and help set clear expectations for deadlines, deliverables, and results. So the next time you get frustrated by someone's poor performance, take for a moment before you say to yourself, *Ugh — he should have known what needs to be done!* Guess what? He probably didn't. This is when you stop yourself and ask, *Did I share what success looks like here? Did I establish the right expectations?* Chances are good that someone's poor performance is a result of something you did *not* do versus something he or she *did* do.

So if you've been able to demonstrate all three aspects of high performance that we've detailed so far — understanding and meeting the standards of others, having a very narrow say-do gap, communicating intent and expectations — this fourth aspect becomes the difference-maker because it brings your team's performance to an entirely new level.

HOLDING OTHERS ACCOUNTABLE WHEN THEY FAIL TO MEET EXPECTATIONS

Sean's Story

In the introduction to this book, I talked about the ready room, the place where flight missions are debriefed after they are completed. After my first debrief experience, when I was admonished for remaining silent, I quickly became comfortable offering performance-related feedback to my colleagues. But as I was promoted in the organization, I knew I would soon find myself working with more senior organizational leaders — specifically, generals who would stay current with their skills by coming down to the squadrons to fly sorties with us. Generals, as you're likely aware, are our organization's equivalent of senior executives. And when you work in a force that has more than 300,000 people and only a handful of generals at the top, you can imagine how awkward it was sometimes to give them candid feedback on their performance.

One morning when I was working as a flight instructor at Luke Air Force Base, I checked out the flight schedule and noticed that my wingman that day was going to be a general. The moment had finally arrived. I've got to tell you, my first emotion was far from excitement. I had never flown with a general before, and I just didn't want to get into the cockpit and feel like my every move was being scrutinized. It would be no different if the CEO of your organization came to shadow you on the job all day. A little unnerving, right?

But as I was coping with this news, I remembered that the general was a regular fighter pilot like me ... only older and more experienced. And if I were in his shoes, I reasoned, I'd want to be treated like all the other pilots. So when he arrived, I planned and briefed the mission to everyone in the room just like we were a group of contemporaries heading out to fly a routine mission.

Once we were finished, we retreated to the ready room and began our debrief in typical fashion by discussing how the team performed together. Then we started to give each other individual feedback. This was when I had to override my desire to *not* give the general the feedback he needed to hear. Truth be told, he was rusty. While I never felt unsafe with him in the cockpit, I knew that if I were to fly with him again, I'd want him to improve on his stick and rudder skills. I thought of all the different ways I could deliver the feedback. I could sugarcoat it, making it seem like it wasn't a big deal. I could serve it up in a compliment sandwich: say something nice, sneak in the constructive criticism, then say something nice again. But then I realized that downplaying the feedback wasn't going to help him get better. He needed to hear the truth directly, so he could improve. Unless I offered it, the problem might persist. I didn't want to be known as the person who glossed over performance problems in the hopes that they would improve miraculously on their own.

So what did I do? I looked the general straight in the eye and told him what I observed and then gave him specific instances where he could have improved. And then I waited for his reaction. And waited. And waited.

When it finally came, what surprised me was that the first words out of his mouth were "Thank you." Then, after agreeing with my feedback, he asked for additional ideas on how to get better. I gave him specific coaching points, and he readily committed to using them in order to improve. When I was done, he expressed a strong desire to get back into the cockpit soon so that he could spend more time getting better. He then started talking about his experiences flying in different airplanes and theaters and about the evolution of flying operations over his career. My colleagues and I spent the rest of the debrief absorbed in his stories, which he wouldn't have told if we hadn't dropped the pretense and shared accountable feedback. We all walked away from this session with lessons learned and a greater confidence in each other because we were able to confront problems with resolve and a commitment to higher performance.

So right now I know that you might be reading this and thinking, *There is no way that I'm going to approach senior leaders in my organization and share with them how they can improve.* And believe me, I'm not advocating for that. At least, not yet.

The idea, though, is that when you develop the courage to deliver performance-based feedback to your colleagues in a way that inspires them to grow from it, you can effectively influence the trust, candor, and performance of your team. And a great place to start bringing accountability to your team is to think about what you can do to spark an honest dialogue on performance. Start by considering the people problems you're experiencing right now and how you could go about addressing them in a productive way.

Maybe one of your colleagues is always late for work, or maybe your direct report doesn't take initiative. Maybe you work with someone who gossips too much in the office or dresses inappropriately. We're never short of problems in our working worlds

—but what we always seem shy of is leaders who are willing to strike up a constructive conversation about what's not working and how it can be improved.

This type of problem-solving could feel counterculture to you. You might work in an organization where accountability is simply absent. Maybe your organization has standards—they're printed in small type in the HR manual—but no one enforces them, so no one follows them. Problems go unaddressed and performance suffers. Or you might work in an organization where managers are the only ones who are responsible for bringing accountability to teams. So when two peers in different departments can't get along, rather than addressing the challenge discreetly and directly, managers swoop in and deliver accountability by discussing standards and expectations with everyone, hoping that the two not meeting them will get the picture.

But in the best organizations—the types that Sparks influence—accountability-based conversations are just part of the organizational DNA. It's not about egos, it's about performance. Here's what it looks like: When there are problems between two colleagues, rather than escalating the situation, they just discuss the missed expectations and work to resolve the problems together. No drama. No mess. A quick conversation, followed by tweaks, and everyone can get back to work with a focus on improving. Sounds utopian, right?

Many participants in our workshops find this type of feedback hard to digest. They challenge, "You want me to tell my colleague where she screwed up? But I'm not her manager." And while that's true, we flip the question. "If someone had a problem with your performance, which would you prefer: that she go to your manager to discuss it or that she come directly to you with it?" After we raise this question, many participants agree, then follow up: "So how do I do this?"

DELIVERING FEEDBACK TO INSPIRE GROWTH

Angie's Story

In the best organizations, everyone knows where they stand. Holding someone accountable is strictly between his or her performance and the expected standard — it's *not* about you and that person personally. It takes Sparks to lead organizations to this point where candor flows freely.

I admit it: delivering feedback is tough if you're not used to doing it. And doing it right takes courage and a healthy dose of tact. It's irresponsible to just let feedback fly without considering its impact. After all, the reason you give feedback is to inspire someone to grow. If you're doing it for any other reason — maybe because you need to be right or you've got an ego to feed — then you're wrong and definitely not the person to offer constructive criticism.

To start building the feedback habit, your focus needs to be on the other person and how you can help him or her. What often prevents us from delivering feedback effectively is spending too much time thinking about ourselves and how we feel about delivering it — like, *I just don't know what to say,* or, *I don't know how I'm going to get through this conversation.* This type of self-focus prevents us from being objective about the situation and getting to a place where we consider the other person and how *they* feel and how *they* would like to hear what we have to say. When you can make feedback about the person *receiving* it, not about the person *delivering* it, you start understanding how to frame your message in a way that inspires, rather than alienates, the recipient. So rather than start a sentence with, "Let me tell you why you're wrong," you might discover that "Hey, let's discuss what just happened there" will prompt a more productive dialogue.

Another idea is to pick your place — make sure you're having a private conversation. You never want to run the risk of embarrassing someone, which can have a negative, lingering effect on your relationship. When I was stationed in Hawaii, I led a team of Marines. One day when I arrived at work at the Command Headquarters Building, I saw two Marines on my team standing at attention while the base sergeant major was ripping them to shreds in a very public place — their colleagues and many senior officers were walking by. While this scene is common in boot camp, it's not that typical in a base environment. I wondered, *What the heck did these lance corporals do to upset the sergeant major?* Surely it had to be serious to get the sergeant major so red in the face. I took it upon myself to break the tension in the situation and find out.

As soon as the sergeant major saw me approach, he stopped his tirade to salute me hastily, which allowed me to salute back and ask, "Sergeant Major, these guys are on my team. What's going on?" He dismissed them quickly, and after they scattered away, he shared that they weren't performing their morning duties to the best of their ability — sweeping the porch to the Command Building, polishing the brass on some of the fixtures, etc. I've got to admit, I was taken aback by that. I wanted to say, "You mean to tell me that their lack of janitorial skills rated that level of humiliation? Dear God, what happens when you really screw up in this organization?" But I held back. I respected the sergeant major's tenure and didn't want to undermine him, so I told him I would take it from there to ensure that the two lance corporals performed their duties to the level of his expectation.

When I saw them a few minutes later to discuss the situation, I found myself talking to two sullen-faced Marines whose confidence was visibly shaken. They were listening to me, nodding in agreement, but were they really thinking about delivering high performance? Were they feeling inspired to be their best? Were they motivated to improve? Hardly. And what about their relationship with the sergeant major? His dressing-down session had damaged their trust in him. These Marines would certainly comply with the sergeant major's requests in the future, but would they approach him with their problems? No. It's human nature to want to avoid pain.

I'd love to say that this type of ranting and berating happens only in the military, but sadly, this happens too often in the private sector. I remember being on-site at a client's office one time and, while waiting in the reception area, I heard screaming coming from a manager's office nearby. A few seconds later, I saw a sullen employee walk out of the office and head to his cubicle. The receptionist looked at me, rolled her eyes, and apologized by saying, "I wish you weren't here to witness this. Someone needs to have a talk with him about his screaming."

Heightened, unharnessed emotions get in the way of feedback, and the message gets lost in the way it's sent. I've even heard people defend their lack of tact: "I expect my team members to take a beating in one meeting," they say, "then turn around and take one in another — they should be more resilient!" We agree: people should be resilient, *and* we shouldn't have to treat each other with kid gloves. But resiliency isn't born out of insults or public shaming. A better approach is to make feedback about the standard and the expectation rather than about the person, and to choose the right tone — one that makes the recipient of the feedback want to take it to heart.

And so it bears repeating: *a leader is someone who influences outcomes and inspires others.* To inspire you have to deliver feedback that doesn't make people cringe and shrink, but motivates them to grow.

After you find the right time and place and have specifically named the standard you'd like to address, the next step is to ask the person if he or she is open to feedback. This is an especially good tactic if that person you're about to give feedback to is your boss or peer. Sometimes a simple conversation starter is, "Hey, I've observed something lately that you might find valuable — are you open to hearing it?" Plus, if the other person says "no," then you know not to proceed. In that case, your feedback probably wouldn't have helped anyway, and you can't command people to change. But if you're giving feedback to one of your direct reports, you don't need this kind of permission — your role as a manager is to deliver feedback and improve your team member's performance!

When you offer your feedback, focus on what you've *observed* and what impact it's had on *you*. Doing this eliminates hearsay. Also, it's more difficult for the other person to get defensive when you're speaking from your point of view. That's not to say the other person won't get defensive — all of us are human, and our egos, which remind us to defend ourselves at all costs, are always at work. What I've learned is that sometimes it's good to remind people, "Hey, this isn't easy for me to say," then round off the conversation with, "Just please consider what I've offered." I also advise not taking the bait if the other person starts hurling insults your way. The last thing you want is an argument. And when you receive feedback yourself during this conversation, take a cue from the general in Sean's story — offer a "thank you."

What we've found is that if you care enough to offer feedback, you also need to have ideas for how the person can improve. There's nothing more annoying than having someone raise an issue without offering any ideas on how to address it. Sparks are problem-solvers, not just problem-spotters.

There are plenty of books and other resources that offer tactics and guidance on framing feedback, and we offer additional information online to help you shape your message. The bottom line, though, is that it's critical to build the feedback habit — do it once and then, as hard as it might feel, keep doing it. And open yourself up to criticism too — one Spark who invites feedback can change an organization where it's been almost taboo and set off an organizational trend of welcoming feedback.

As we've shared in this chapter, Sparks are committed to bettering themselves and others. When you start to speak up about problems, you'll grow more comfortable doing so in the future. And as a result, you'll find that the teams you're a part of are less focused on petty issues and more focused on high performance, because everyone is working toward the same goal.

SPARK ACTIONS

To be a credible Spark, you have to commit yourself to the following four keys to credibility:

- Understand the expectations others have for you — other people often have unspoken standards they're measuring your performance against.
- Mind your say-do gap — often we undermine our influence by not following through on the commitments we make.
- Let others know what's expected of them — by giving others a clear picture of what success looks like, you're helping them contribute to the credibility of their team.
- Have the courage to deliver performance-related feedback to others — when delivered effectively, feedback can be the most valuable thing you do for your colleagues.

CHARGING AHEAD

Your credibility is your on-ramp to greater influence with others, and it's too important to be left to chance. Start purposefully developing it and you'll soon discover that your performance is stronger and you're in a better position to be the go-to person sought out by others. We're here to help you explore this topic further with the following exercises on www.sparkslead.us:

- *Stakeholders:* Have you ever wondered what others expect of you and what standards they're measuring you against? This exercise will help you consider the perspective of key stakeholders and understand how you can be more credible in their eyes.
- *Say-Do Gap:* Do you think your team suffers from a wide say-do gap? This exercise, designed to get groups discussing the inconsistencies between their actions and their words, helps individuals — and teams — generate positive discussions on credibility.
- *Culture of Accountability:* It might seem unrealistic to work in an environment where positive and developmental feedback flows freely, but you can be the catalyst for this type of exchange in your organization. This exercise allows you to start the dialogue with your team.

Once you make the effort to recognize the actions you can take to strengthen your credibility, move on to the next chapter on accountable leaders. As you'll soon read, being accountable is another one of those head games requiring that you override some powerful instincts that might be holding you back and keeping you from getting to where you want to go.

4

BECOMING AN
ACCOUNTABLE LEADER

Sparks who demonstrate accountability resist the powerful human instinct to place blame elsewhere. They seek to identify how their own actions — or inactions — have contributed to the situations in which they find themselves.

IN THE LAST CHAPTER, we talked about how accountability requires you to bring up problems you observe among others. Letting errors or poor workmanship slide is not, of course, leadership behavior. However, looking elsewhere for improvement opportunities is only part of being a Spark. The other part involves self-evaluation. Is it possible that *you* are part of the problem? You're human, after all. When you make mistakes, miss expectations, or are a part of a team that doesn't make the cut, how do you handle these critically important moments? If you are a Spark, you are accountable.

Demonstrating accountability means relentlessly seeking ownership of mistakes, missteps, problems, and any other less-than-best outcome you are either responsible for or associated with. Accountability is not about conducting a witch hunt to figure out who did what wrong and what should happen to them. When demonstrated correctly, accountability is the acknowledgment — *not the admiration* — of a mistake and quickly moving beyond it to get to what everyone wants: the solution and resolution.

It takes courage and willpower for Sparks to take personal responsibility for those challenges or errors they created or in which they took part. But if there's a problem and they're close enough to it, Sparks are accountable, and as a result, they distinguish themselves as problem-solvers, truth-brokers, and confidence-inspiring leaders. One lone Spark can transform a blame-placing group into a results-oriented team that is shaping its future. That is the powerful impact that Sparks can have.

But demonstrating accountability isn't easy. Some powerful forces are working against us when we attempt to be our best in trying moments.

This includes our stress response, which is a *physiological reaction* we experience when we feel threatened. It's our body's reaction to a stressor, whatever it is. When there's a problem, it's natural to want to fight, flee, or freeze. Like when your manager tells you that you missed your sales quota by 15 percent. In that moment, you're not thinking, *You're right. I* didn't *put the effort into last quarter.* Instead, your instincts are to defend your performance and, possibly, pin your shortcoming on someone or something else—like the ridiculous quota set by corporate or the challenging market conditions. Acting on instinctive behavior or becoming defensive in effect pushes you further away from the result you're accountable for.

We also have our ego to contend with when we're trying to be accountable. When faced with problems that embarrass us or cause us anxiety, we experience *psychological reactions* that prevent us from being a Spark. Like when a colleague informs you that the tone you used in a companywide email was inappropriate, your instinct might be either to blame the sensitive employees working at your company (ignoring the insensitivity of the person who sent the email) or to defend your behavior in an attempt to prove that you're right and *they're* wrong. Again, acting on your instincts is likely not only to perpetuate the problem but also to damage your relationship with your colleague.

We're clearly not hardwired to be accountable when we feel challenged, but that's no reason why we can't learn to override our instincts and be a Spark during these critical moments. We absolutely can. It starts with being able to identify these critical moments when real accountability is needed in your life. And here's a hint: these moments usually happen when you're experiencing considerable frustration and things just aren't going your way.

THE ACCOUNTABILITY MOMENT

Angie's Story

What often stands between us and the better life we envision is our ability to accept responsibility for our role in our situation and work harder to achieve a better result. I know this because I experienced it firsthand when I was a young second lieutenant at The Basic School, the first formal school I attended as a Marine.

Until TBS, I had had a string of successes. I graduated at the top of my Naval Reserve Officer Training Corps (NROTC) and my OCS classes, I was selected for a prestigious leadership organization at the University of Michigan, and I received a leadership award from the university's president. But as soon as I arrived at TBS I went from superstar to struggling performer in an instant.

It began on day one of TBS when our instructors introduced the massive syllabus. Our training up until then had focused on physical and mental endurance. This was now our time to focus on the technical and tactical aspects of troop leadership so we could lead Marines in combat. Every activity was new to me, and I was baffled from the get-go by all the new words, concepts, and ideas. It was truly like learning a different language.

When our instructors talked about weaponry, I was lost. I knew nothing about rifles, guns, or the differences between the two. But when I looked around at my colleagues, I saw them nodding and asking insightful questions while they kept pace with the instruction. *How do they know all this stuff?* I couldn't help but wonder.

Then we'd go out on the rifle range, where we all had to qualify with an M-16 rifle and M-9 pistol at various distances, using a variety of different techniques. Let's just say firing weapons wasn't my strength, as evidenced by my fairly low marksman score.

And then there was land navigation: we were dropped deep into the woods by helicopter and had to navigate toward different checkpoints using only a map and a compass. Again, total failure. I didn't pass the first test, but fortunately, I was given an opportunity to retake it. I passed the second time, but not by much.

This was the first time in my life I was absolutely terrible at everything I attempted to do. I would drive home from training each night rattled because I felt like such a loser and I didn't know how to respond. But, oh, my ego did. And it was working overtime to help me deal with these setbacks, failures, and missed expectations.

In truth, my ego always had an excuse for my poor performance. *I'm a girl—I just wasn't socialized in my younger years around weaponry like my male colleagues were. My rifle is too large for my petite frame, and the pistol doesn't sit comfortably in my small hands. My compass never works—it freezes up whenever I'm in the woods.* I was never short of excuses, but always shy of results.

And just when I thought life couldn't get worse for me, it was peer evaluation time, when your colleagues write anonymous evaluations of your performance and leadership potential. Considering my performance level up to this point in training, I wasn't expecting high marks. But that being said, I also wasn't prepared to hear what I did.

My platoon commander, a Marine Corps captain, called me into his office to review my evals. He showed me the list of words my colleagues used to describe me. Sure, there were favorable comments, but the negative ones stood out: "Self-absorbed, insincere, inconsistent, selfish, etc." My first thoughts were, *Whoa — who is this person? Is this me? How can this be me?*

My captain picked up on my distress and asked for my reaction. I knew I had to come clean. I told him my struggles, my concerns, and how I felt about my performance. I confided that the words used to describe me were painfully accurate. I did spend more time thinking about myself and less about my team. I also shared that this was the most challenging thing I had ever done, and that I was concerned about how credible I was going to be when I had to lead Marines.

At this point, the captain offered me a perspective I needed to consider as well as a lifeline I had no choice but to take. He said that I wasn't the first person to come to his office with these confessions. The purpose of TBS was to train you — not just on technical skills. The role of the Marine Corps was to support me as I transformed into a leader. He smiled and said, "This part is called 'accountability.' You need to be responsible for your performance — only you can do that. And only you have the power to improve your performance by gaining the support of your colleagues, your instructors, and me. We will be accountable for your success. You will fail yourself before we will fail you. And that's the beauty of the Marine Corps — we won't fail you. Let's get you on a remedial path in training. It's going to require extra work and effort, but let's ensure that the second half of this training is much better than the first." And with his support, not only did my training record improve, but my attitude and outlook did as well.

The captain served as an important mentor at a critical time in my young career. By providing me with a strong accountability message during my time of need, he gave me a framework for dealing with these challenges. And later on, when I would face the inevitable bumps in both my personal life and my professional career, I was better prepared to handle them because he had taught me the secret skill set for navigating through the down moments. I needed to accept responsibility for my own actions and their ramifications. That's what Sparks do. They serve as role models for others by being accountable for everything they do, good and bad.

Now, that's not to say that being accountable is an easy thing to do — hardly. There is some pain involved (and some pride that may have to get swallowed).

I've since realized that most professionals don't get the benefit of this type of accountability messaging when they're in the gutter, so to speak. When most people experience low points, others surround them either to vindicate or to validate them. "You're right — the organization was out to get you! Your company is a terrible place to work." Or, "I agree — your boss is a jerk! You had every right to tell him off."

The problem is, this is invariably poor advice. We need to accept responsibility when the chips are down and be supported by our environments to help us get the results we seek. But unfortunately, these types of environments seem to be the exception — not the norm.

SO WHY IS ACCOUNTABILITY SO RARE?

Whenever we deliver a workshop and ask our audience if they're satisfied with the level of accountability they experience, heads shake from side to side. It would appear that accountability is in short supply today.

Overwhelmingly, we all seem to agree that we live in a pass-the-buck culture. Pointing to others as the reason for a problem is a typical response. We blame the teacher when our child is failing, the fast-food restaurants for making us fat, and the credit card companies for driving us into debt. The problem always lies elsewhere. It's never our fault. Blaming someone else has become the cultural norm.

Blaming someone or something else might not hurt you in the moment, but it also doesn't help. Your challenges won't get better until you fully accept your role in the situations that create them. Your strained relationship with your in-laws, for example, is only partially the fault of your spouse's parents. You are partly to blame as well. That means *you* are also part of the problem, but the good news is that you have the power to alter that dynamic.

If you keep getting passed over for a promotion, maybe it's not the hiring manager's fault. There is something you can do to take ownership of your situation. It might be uncomfortable reflecting on your weaknesses and the reasons you're being passed over, but it is truly the only way to identify and accept responsibility for the root cause of the problem and formulate a solution going forward. You may have to make some changes, and you might even have to consider transitioning to another company, but until you can become accountable, you can't begin to problem-solve. That's the difference with Sparks — they look for a way around the roadblock in front of them, whatever it is, and don't try to pass the buck on to someone else.

This approach benefited a colleague of ours in a pretty significant way. When Patrick Nelson transitioned out of the Army, he felt assured that his military success would position him well in the private sector. He had led teams in combat, been deployed multiple times overseas, and been responsible for equipment that totaled millions of dollars. He had been given tremendous responsibility at such an early stage in his career and had been awarded for his service, including a Bronze Star for meritorious service in combat and a Purple Heart for injuries he sustained in a rocket attack on a helicopter landing zone. He was — and still is — the kind of guy you want on your team to see results through at all costs. Somehow, though, his experiences as they were written out on paper didn't match employers' needs.

After sending out more than eighty résumés — even to fast-food restaurants that had NOW HIRING signs posted on their message boards — and getting zero callbacks, Patrick was at a loss. As tempting as it was to blame businesses for not valuing his service, he knew that wouldn't help him. Patrick chose to channel his energy into a more productive pursuit.

Rather than get angry or mad, he decided to develop experiences that would make his résumé more attractive to prospective employers. He started by going to college to pursue a bachelor's degree and taking on a part-time job to develop a business background. And once he discovered that he wanted a career in sports management, he applied for — and was later awarded — the first-ever NFL–Pat Tillman Military Scholarship, and he also became a Horatio Alger Scholar. Upon completion of his master's degree, he landed a dream job: a role with the Minnesota Vikings. All this occurred because he chose to be better than his instincts. Instead of lamenting the lack of job offers, Patrick took action — he took responsibility — to enhance his credentials. He reviewed the results he was achieving with his current approach and background, brainstormed solutions to the problem of getting no callbacks, and arrived at a college degree as the stepping-stone to landing his dream job. That's Spark behavior.

We're not born accountable leaders. A three-year-old who is caught stealing a cookie red-handed does not immediately own up to his role in the problem; he points the finger at his little sister. Not a lot changes as we grow into adults. We certainly pick up on rules and cues about how to respond in socially acceptable ways, but our instincts — those physiological and psychological reactions we just discussed — grow old with us. When we feel those heightened emotions — as we do when something's wrong or our mistakes have caught up with us — we often find ourselves making excuses, blaming others, or concocting elaborate scenarios to try to cover up our poor decision-making. When we do this, we create distance between our goals and ourselves. Others even lose respect for us because they observe our problems, see our reactions, and aren't influenced or inspired by how we respond in those moments when our personal accountability is needed.

But we can learn to develop personal accountability by focusing on cognitive discipline, which we described earlier as our ability to inhibit our instincts and choose a less obvious, but more effective, response — *a learned leadership response*. A Spark response.

When we pay attention to them, our instincts clue us in that it is our leadership skills — not our knee-jerk reactions — that are needed to improve a situation.

And the more in tune we are with our behaviors, the more mindful we can be in managing them, and the more inspiring we can be during those moments when we're being challenged to pass the accountability test.

The accountability test doesn't come to you in the moments when you're prepared for it — you know, those moments when you're well rested, you've studied your notes, and you feel entirely confident that you're going to pass the test. Nope, the accountability test comes at you when you're emotionally vulnerable, scared, and confused. But it's in these dire moments that you can emerge as a Spark and set the tone for how to address challenges courageously. When you can model this level of accountability, you create the conditions for high performance on whatever teams you are a part of.

ONE ACCOUNTABLE LEADER INSPIRES OTHERS

Sean's Story

I can attest that when you're surrounded by accountable leaders, you're inspired to be accountable too.

Even if that means admitting a mistake that could end your career.

When I was stationed in Korea, our mission was to defend the Thirty-Eighth Parallel, which forms a boundary between North Korea and our ally, South Korea. Part of our work in Korea was practicing air-to-air tactics involving four F-16s — two versus two. Preparation for such a mission started on the ground with checking all the aircraft's systems, such as flight controls and radar, as well as your own G-suit, which was designed to keep you alive during high-gravity flight. The suit itself wraps around your legs and abdomen, squeezing your body to keep blood from pooling in your legs so oxygen can flow to your brain.

One memorable day during a routine exercise, I completely checked out the plane but forgot to check my G-suit, which was not connected into the aircraft pressurization system. For whatever reason, I missed it that day — a horrendous and potentially perilous oversight on my part. And then, when I was given a second chance to test my gear — by performing two 90-degree turns designed to confirm that our G-suits were inflating properly — I didn't notice that mine wasn't. My colleagues and I proceeded to our training mission, which was to lock our radar onto an opposing jet in a very close, very visual, dogfight.

To succeed in getting behind the other jet and employing our weapons, we had to turn sharply, hitting 9 G's in less than a second. As we did that I blacked out — I lost consciousness at an altitude of 25,000 feet while in control of a $40 million aircraft that was flying extremely close — dangerously close — to other jets.

When I started to come to a couple of seconds later, I felt like I was in the middle of a dream, surrounded by fuzzy airplanes. But then the other jets started to come into focus and a wave of panic, confusion, and alarm swept over me as I realized I wasn't at home in bed.

"Knock it off!" I said into my radio, delivering the protocol command that alerts the other pilots to abort the mission immediately and to head back to base.

I had just put my life, the lives of others, and many millions of dollars' worth of military equipment at risk with my careless oversight. I was beyond embarrassed by my critical error. During my flight back to base, my mind raced through worst-case scenarios about what would happen to me when I told my colleagues about what I had failed to do. Was I going to get demoted? Was I going to get fired? I had no way of knowing, but I was prepared to accept my fate.

There was no way I could pretend I hadn't screwed up, and my team needed to know what happened. I had to be honest so my fellow pilots would know that they could continue to count on me. They had to know I would be honest even at the risk of embarrassment, personal pride, or career jeopardy.

Admitting my mistake to my team wasn't easy. But what was surprising was how appreciative they were that I was so forthcoming. We used my error as an opportunity to talk about accident prevention, and we even discussed whether or not we had the right checks in place to ensure that this type of mistake never happened again. My boss shared later that when you initiate accountability, you inspire trust. It's trying to cover up your mistakes or shirk responsibility that gets you in trouble — it can even get you kicked out of the Air Force.

The Air Force environment I worked in promoted accountability throughout the organization and was very different from most organizations I've since been a part of. After leaving the military, I became a commercial pilot and had to work routinely with a number of different airline businesses that demonstrated varying degrees of accountability. In some organizations, it seemed acceptable to throw colleagues under the bus when problems arose — like blaming a supervisor's poor planning when the catering company arrived late to restock the aircraft. In other organizations, it was even appropriate to blame history for poor performance — "We've always treated passengers this way! When did they decide they didn't like it?" And in some organizations accountability meant trouble, so no one wanted to demonstrate it. When you admit you're wrong, there is a good chance you'll encounter backlash and ridicule, even be used as the corporatewide cautionary tale. "Don't do that! Tom once did that and, boy, what a mess he caused for himself!"

Our mistakes can cost money and time, inconvenience others, damage relationships, and the list goes on. But Sparks have the courage to face the consequences and handle them responsibly. When we do, we show others who we are and what we're made of. And we keep our leadership reputation intact.

We once worked with the chief executive officer of a small business who was having disagreements with his board of directors. The board ended up firing him, leaving him disappointed, confused, and concerned about his career. Still, he worked hard to manage his emotions and accepted the company's decision with real grace. The board was genuinely surprised, and perhaps a little relieved. So much so that board members wrote a glowing letter of recommendation for the former CEO and even tapped into their networks to help him find new job opportunities. None of this would have happened had the CEO reacted negatively to this challenging scenario.

In addition to being accountable, Sparks often have to create opportunities for accountability to happen. Let's face it, most people don't come to meetings ready to air their problems. Many of our clients have boardrooms — but none have ready rooms, where problems are openly discussed. The intense pace within so many organizations prevents discussion of problems, eliminating any opportunity to address them, learn from them, and make improvements accordingly. It's similar to what happens in twenty-four-hour operations at shift changes. When the 2:00–10:00 p.m. crew turns over to the 10:00 p.m.–6:00 a.m. crew, the conversations typically relate to picking up operations, not dissecting challenges related to process or personnel. Or in professional services companies, where professionals get so focused on billables that they don't take the time to challenge the way they interact or engage with their colleagues and clients. It's easy in any organization to develop tunnel vision.

On your Spark journey, the best way to go about promoting accountability is by creating operational pauses for conversation — a chance to debrief and to discuss issues. If you're in the middle of executing an ad campaign, pull your colleagues together to discuss where you are, what's happening, what's going well, and what needs to be improved. This type of reflection allows you to calibrate your own actions moving forward as the team addresses any problems preventing it from achieving its goals. And if you're also forthcoming about your own challenges, you create a safe place for others to be accountable too. When others share their mistakes and missteps, you don't need to beat them up — believe me, all of us, as humans, do a great job of that on our own. Help them get to the action steps they need to apply going forward. That's where the learning happens and that's how performance is driven.

BUILDING THE HABIT

Being a Spark requires that you have the courage to put yourself or your reputation in harm's way. But once you do it, you will find the courage to do it again. And before you know it, you're building solid Spark habits and inspiring excellence from your colleagues across your organization.

When organizations are comprised of Sparks, they're free of blame-placing or getting lost in arguments on who did what, how, and why. Rather, they are focused on being nimble, responding to challenges, and focusing on the future. They're also tackling problems they didn't create, not avoiding them, because they have the mindset to be proactive, not reactive, in the face of pressing issues. The "blame game" and other behaviors that have nothing to do with accountability take up too much time — time that is needed to focus on results.

When a client of ours took over as executive director of a nonprofit workforce development organization in southwestern Michigan in 2005, he was responsible for transforming the way his organization engaged in job creation in the community they served. He realized that his first order of business was to address the cultural mindset of his team members, who were more focused on what they could *not* do to serve their community than on what they *could* do. Whenever he pressed his team to be creative in their approach to their work, a litany of excuses would ensue. Team members would complain that their hands were tied because the state government was so restrictive on grants, or they'd explain that they "tried that before and it didn't work" as a way to defend the status quo; they would even state that they would gladly initiate action if only it was in their job description. The lack of accountability had his organization mired in the past and was keeping them ill equipped to prepare for the future.

Our client wasn't discouraged, but he recognized that he had a journey ahead of him. He began by introducing leadership training throughout the entire organization to get his team thinking about themselves as leaders and creating an accountability mindset to help them address their challenges. Not everyone was excited about undergoing leadership development, but the process allowed him to find the Sparks in his organization who were motivated to lead. As Sparks emerged, he placed them in key positions where they'd have greater influence. What he observed over time was the total transformation of a team — from one that was inattentive to results to one that saw opportunities to expand their mission to better serve their community. This led to the creation of an entirely new organization, which now serves as a national model for business, workforce, and community development.

The presence of accountability allowed our client's organization to thrive. And for many businesses, accountability is the only way they can survive. This was especially the case for our firm, Lead Star, when we were navigating through the Great Recession of 2008. It could be the same case for many organizations, recession or not, especially considering the rate of change many firms are experiencing in our dynamic, and sometimes disruptive, working world.

ACCOUNTABILITY DRIVES HIGH PERFORMANCE

Courtney's Story

Small businesses can serve as great case studies for smaller units or divisions within large businesses. Our firm has some convincing evidence to show that when teams are accountable, they can respond to changing market conditions in a way that sets them up for long-term success.

When Angie and I created Lead Star in our late twenties, sheer ambition and scrappiness got our business off the ground. (And of course, so did our willingness to combine our savings and max out our credit cards to come up with the capital to invest in our dreams.) Our hard work and commitment paid off: our firm grew exponentially as our loyal client base consistently referred us to other businesses. Angie and I traveled regularly to *Fortune* 500 clients to deliver leadership development presentations while our managing director ran the business in our absence. This pace was as exhilarating as it was exhausting for our small, but mighty, team.

After our first book hit bookstores, we knew we needed to do something to capture all the opportunities that were in front of us. So we decided to bring in a salesperson to manage client relationships and pursue new contracts. That way, we thought, the two of us could focus solely on our training programs, rather than sales, and maybe even reduce some of our workload.

Our new team member came with a track record of success and achievement. It was clear that she knew how to sell, so naturally we had high hopes for what her talents could do for our firm.

With the sales function addressed, Angie and I turned our attention to developing new programs. We had scores of satisfied clients, so we thought our next step should be to create new products and services to sell them. We forged ahead with creating new offerings.

But it wasn't long before we saw signs that all was not well.

Our first tip-off was that people had stopped signing up for our open enrollment training events, such as our Leadership Boot Camp. Typically, registrations would be slow at first and then ramp up as the date drew near. Suddenly, no one was signing up at all. Seeing that set off alarm bells in our heads. We depended on that revenue for operating costs. Then we noticed that our third quarter 2008 sales were half of what they had been the prior year. The economy was also in a nosedive, and corporate training budgets were being slashed. Clients called us frequently to express their frustrations over not being able to follow through on their training commitments. We were stressed and overwhelmed as we witnessed our sales forecast collapse in front of our eyes. We began to worry about what would happen if the business failed. Could we go back to corporate jobs? How would we ever cover our business debt?

We were desperate, but we knew we couldn't act irrationally. This was our moment to make some tough choices to account for the challenges we found ourselves facing. To continue to support the business, Angie and I suspended our salary payments to make payroll for our team members. We met frequently to discuss our options and sought counsel from our mentors. We knew we had to get to the root of the problem quickly or our business would be no more.

We also had to have the discipline *not* to place blame. Stress has a funny way of bringing out unhealthy, unproductive emotions. It would have been so easy to start pointing fingers at our salesperson. With sales dramatically lower, clearly she was not doing her job, we could have said. We could have also blamed the economy: we were just like any other small business that was about to become a recession casualty. We could have even blamed each other; after all, a business partnership is like a marriage — you are always working together, and when things aren't going smoothly, you wonder if your partner is working as hard as you are to ensure success.

This is where our leadership training in the Marine Corps was invaluable. We knew we had to avoid placing blame and instead evaluate our own roles in the situation. When we looked hard at where we were, we recognized that we were using the wrong business model. We had approached the sales process like we were running a consumer products business when in fact we were a professional services firm. Ultimately, our sales process really should have been more like a law firm model, where partners are responsible for attracting and signing new clients and a marketing director provides support. The truth was, our clients wanted to deal with the two of us *personally*. They wanted to meet and interact with the consultant providing services. By placing our salesperson in between the clients and ourselves, we had prolonged our sales cycle and ended up frustrating our clients. Our sales rep was fantastic, but she could not have overcome this flaw — a flaw we had not seen.

So we did what needed to be done. We had an honest, difficult conversation with our salesperson in which we all agreed that the arrangement wasn't working for any of us. We gave her a glowing reference, and she landed an amazing position where she blew her sales quota out of the water immediately. Angie and I had assessed what we had done wrong and discovered what we needed to do to get back on course. We started reaching out to previous clients and networking with new ones. We researched industries that had not been as affected by the recession and had training budgets and subsequently landed a number of high-profile tech and social media clients.

By taking responsibility and focusing our attention on sales, we turned our situation around quickly. We actually ended 2008 with 6.2 percent growth over 2007, rebounding from the 50 percent drop in third-quarter sales. The following year we saw 49.8 percent growth and higher profitability. By being accountable, we were willing to face our mistakes and to learn what needed to be done. The experience also helped us become more resilient. Overall, it was a tough and frightening lesson to learn, but one that we couldn't walk away from.

We recognize that no one can always anticipate what next challenge is waiting around the corner. But all of us can constantly build our adaptive capacity by focusing on being accountable in our daily interactions. By continuously examining our mistakes, discussing problems openly, and applying hard lessons learned, we ensure that we continuously grow from our mistakes. The more consistent your ability to be accountable becomes, the more consistent success becomes for you and the teams you are a part of.

SPARK ACTIONS

To be an accountable Spark:

- Lead with accountability so that you're modeling the behavior you expect from others.

- Seek to recognize and embrace problems. Don't deny them, ignore them, or wait for them to come to you. The sooner you address problems, the sooner you achieve the results you're looking for.
- Work to ensure that the teams you work on allow for mistakes. The best teams discuss problems openly and apply their learnings going forward.

CHARGING AHEAD

Being accountable isn't always easy, but it's incredibly rewarding. While you may have some powerful, instinctual forces working against you when problems arise, you can learn to overcome them by not being reactive in challenging situations but consciously choosing your response.

We believe that your quickest path to becoming a Spark is through your ability to be accountable. We've created the following resources on www.sparkslead.us to help you understand how to become more accountable in your own life:

- *Accountability Grid:* Accountability solves problems. To understand the problems you'd like to address, start examining the challenges you experience, what you can control about them, and how you can proactively address the situation. This exercise helps you understand that when you focus on the actions you can take rather than on what you can't control, you're closer to the success you want to realize.
- *Team Accountability:* What problems are holding your team back? This focused exercise allows your team to identify the challenges they're experiencing that are limit-

ing their performance. It also can be used to help teams brainstorm about what they can do to seek and implement solutions.

After you've had the chance to reflect on the actions you can take to address the challenges you experience, you'll be ready for the next chapter — on acting with intent.

5

ACT WITH INTENT: MAKE DECISIONS THAT MATTER

By having a clear vision and making choices consistent with it, Sparks achieve the success they seek. They recognize that seemingly small choices today will have a big impact on the fulfillment they desire for their future.

YOU ARE THE SUM of your decisions. The quality of your life, the strength of your relationships, the stress level you experience, and your career satisfaction are all a result of every choice you've made up to this point in life.

So how are you doing?

As you reflect, first think of all your great accomplishments before turning your attention to work left undone. When you look toward the horizon, what do you see? What are you doing intentionally right now to achieve the vision you have for yourself, personally *and* professionally?

Visions are valuable. It's always good to take the time to think through your life and career and to move toward your goals. Why? Because life is always full of unexpected twists and turns, and unless you have a true sense of where you want to go, you'll find yourself going in circles. Sure, you'll be busy as you keep going in circles, but motion doesn't equal progress.

Sparks are the thinkers and the doers who envision what a better future looks like and take actions that lead themselves — and others — toward it. The "action" piece is key. There are plenty of dreamers in this world who've never honored their ideas with effort. Sparks differentiate themselves by having the discipline and the fortitude to execute, even when they aren't sure what to do next. This allows them to lead their lives and careers, initiate the change they'd like to see for themselves and others, and experience the success that is meaningful to them.

This all sounds great, right? So what stands between us and our ability to be a Spark? Typically, it is any one of the following challenges:

- Failing to envision what a better life could look like
- Falling into routines that bog us down (and prevent us from being a Spark)
- Not making decisions that advance us toward our goals

Fortunately, all of these challenges can be overcome with the right strategies in place.

LACK OF VISION

Sean's Story

When I was in my midforties, I found myself in a rut, though from afar it looked like I had everything. A beautiful wife, two amazing kids, and a house with a pool near the coast in Florida. Having acquired twenty-three years in the cockpit, I also had a career most pilots would have envied. But if you had shadowed me for a week to observe my reality, you would've seen that a pilot's life is far from glamorous. Each week I would drive to the airport in my economy car (sorry, no motorcycle), get on a shuttle bus, walk through security, and hop on a plane. I would then arrive at my destination, hop on another shuttle bus, and sleep in some random hotel. Contrary to stereotypes, I didn't go to wild parties with my colleagues: I went to bed . . . and then woke up early to read the newspaper.

During these slow mornings on the road, I'd spend a lot of time thinking about my family back at home. Then, before I knew it, it was time to put my uniform on and start the whole process again.

Like many professionals, I got caught up in the routine. It was familiar and secure, and my family and I had built our life around it. But was it fulfilling? I guess that wasn't a question I'd asked myself because it felt, at the time, unimportant. And frankly, I didn't really have a vision for how my life could be different. I was focused on having a stable career — one that could support my family's lifestyle — rather than on a career that would progress or evolve. And with the piloting skills I had been developing my whole adult life, I couldn't envision how to apply them elsewhere. Until, of course, I talked with Courtney.

People ask us all the time if we're married because we share the same last name. We're not married, but we're related — she married my kid brother. During one of our family get-togethers, I overheard Courtney talking to my other sister-in-law about Lead Star and the success her firm was experiencing. This caught my attention.

"What do you do again?" I interjected. And then I listened, and before I knew it I was captivated. Courtney was traveling around the country, meeting talented professionals, and designing and delivering training programs for some pretty impressive organizations. It sounded like fun — a lot more fun than what I was doing. I pushed her for more details — "What aspects of leadership do you cover? ... What does a typical training program look like? ... What clients do you work with?" And soon we were swapping military stories on how we had learned leadership and how we've since applied it.

As we wrapped up our conversation, Courtney raised a question that really got me thinking: "Sean, have you ever thought of being a trainer? I think you'd be great at it!" My first thought was that I've trained before — in fact, I've trained throughout my career. One of my favorite things to do in the Air Force was train new pilots and give them guidance on how to succeed in squadron life. I also spent time at Delta Airlines helping other pilots whenever new initiatives were rolled out. Up until that moment, I'd never considered that training had been an integral part of my career; clearly, my assessment of my skills was one-dimensional.

Courtney had opened a window that allowed me to see that there was an entirely different career possibility for me, and surprisingly, I was eager to learn more. At the end of our talk, I said, "Hey, keep me in mind if there's ever an opportunity and you need someone to help you out."

And wouldn't you know it, she called a few weeks later to share that she and Angie had a training class at Marine Corps Base Quantico for civilian employees on communication skills. Would I happen to be available to facilitate it? After learning more about the topics the course would be presenting, I felt like the training would be a great fit because it would leverage my background and experiences. I jumped at the chance and was ready to do whatever it took to prepare. (Preparation wasn't just learning the curriculum, of course — I also needed to be prepared for all the Air Force jokes that were going to be tossed my way. Marines, who are definitely the most physical of all the services, love to joke about the lack of physicality in Air Force training — or rather, "Chair Force" training. I was going to have to learn some good Marine Corps jokes to toss right back at them.)

When Courtney sent me the facilitator guide, she also sent me a schedule to follow that would ensure I'd be ready to deliver the course. On the first day of executing the schedule, what surprised me was how nervous I was. I felt like I was studying for a big final exam. I was learning something new, which would have been exciting enough in itself, but what was special about this moment was seeing myself do something that I'd never imagined before. It was exhilarating.

When the workshop day finally came, I was more than prepared. As I was getting ready on the morning of the event, it dawned on me that this was the first time in my adult life I didn't need to put on a uniform to perform my job — I didn't even have to wear a matching hat. And then, when I arrived at the classroom, I met a bunch of people who, unlike so many airline passengers preparing for a five-hour flight, had smiling faces and were eager for the day ahead.

The training session lasted only one day, but it gave me just enough time to realize that I had found a new career. It's funny to think about this now, but I consider this my own re-Sparking moment. I called Courtney immediately after my session to discuss how the day went and did my best to try to keep it cool as I shared with her the strong evaluations that attendees gave me (even though I was feeling elated, like I had just aced the SATs).

I then called my wife and let her know that this was the first time in a very long time that I felt a real sense of excitement about going to work. "Don't get me wrong," I said, "flying an airplane can be fun. But I've just been doing it for so long. This training stuff is new and rewarding in an entirely different way than piloting."

As Angie and Courtney continued to build their business, they would give me a call when they ran into challenges and needed an independent contractor to deliver courses. When this started happening more frequently, we all agreed that maybe it was time for me to join their team. Ever since I accepted their offer, I really can't envision doing anything else.

Looking back, I recognize now that my "stuck in a rut" feeling was really a lack of vision. Even though I jumped headfirst into piloting when I was in college, somewhere along the way in my twenty-three-year career as a pilot I became so focused on putting one foot in front of the other that I forgot to pick my head up to see what trail I was on. I also know I'm not the only person who has had this experience. I've met many professionals who say, "I haven't put a lot of planning into my career. Opportunities pop up and I just accept them." That sounds a lot like what happened with me. Both in the Air Force and with the airlines, once you sign on you march, lockstep, in and out of roles and responsibilities. It's pretty easy to just wait and be told what to do and where to go next without stopping to consider your personal vision for yourself and what you'd like to do next. I often think about where I'd be — and the goals I'd have accomplished — had I acted more intentionally with my career more than a decade ago. I don't have regrets. I just have a little curiosity, but that's why as a parent I'm adamant with my kids that they explore a wide range of options before settling into any one decision.

Now that I'm with Lead Star and I've had a chance to observe different professionals from different industries who have experienced varying degrees of success, it's clear to me that the most satisfied and engaged people are those who are truly leading and taking charge of their careers. These are the Sparks — those who respect the career paths laid out for them, but who also value their own personal vision for where they want to take their career. The bottom line is that you need a vision to stay motivated. It allows you to stay focused and helps you avoid feeling disengaged. Better yet, it also helps you go from just accepting opportunities to actually creating them, and that brings about a whole new level of success.

But all this being said, I also fully respect that a personal vision, while incredibly valuable, can be quite challenging to imagine, to develop, and to execute.

IMAGINING YOUR FUTURE

Many of us have a hard time imagining our future. And especially as we get older, we also underestimate how much change we have left to experience. Harvard social psychologist Dan Gilbert calls this the End of History Illusion, which he describes in one of his TED talks. Gilbert shares that we can appreciate how much we've grown over the years, but that we also assume the person we are today is the person we'll be in the future. While we may not change as much as we did between the ages of ten and twenty, there's still a lot of growth left between the ages of forty and sixty. In other words, we should by no means consider ourselves finished products. We are still very much works in progress.

When we buy into the End of History Illusion, we limit our potential by not considering the possibility of new goals or major changes. As a result, we might miss out on key opportunities to become Sparks because we fail to be leaders in our own career and life. New hires who don't look three years into the future and envision where they'd like to be probably won't take real and intentional action *today* in their career development. A researcher who feels stuck in the same dead-end job, in the same dismal location, isn't imagining how things could — and should — be better and therefore isn't doing anything to make it so. That's most unfortunate.

The goal isn't necessarily to have a crystal-clear vision of how your life should be at every twist and turn. A vision is more of an idea of what you're striving toward and an opportunity to raise the expectations you have for yourself and for others.

Be cautious, though, before you jump right in and start thinking up too many big, bold dreams. You need to put a framework around your thinking before you fall victim to "choice overload." Too many choices, too many possibilities, can be dizzying and overwhelming and produce unintended consequences — such as making you cling to the status quo when staying the same is exactly what you're trying to avoid.

Researcher Barry Schwartz calls this the Paradox of Choice. As he explains in his book, *The Paradox of Choice: Why More Is Less,* we become anxious when we have too many decisions to make, and this can make us feel unwanted pressure. We fear that, faced with too many choices, we'll make the wrong one, that we'll choose a direction that leads us astray. So we end up going with the safe path we're familiar with, which is like walking into an ice cream parlor that has fifty different flavors and always settling on vanilla because that was your favorite flavor as a child. Or deciding to buy a new car and then, after brief research, just choosing the newer model of your old car. Not that these choices are wrong — but chances are they could be better.

There is a solid way to put some real structure around your vision of your future so that you can think big and define a direction. It starts with thinking about your specific goals, your interests, and the things you've always wanted to do — like living overseas, freelancing, or taking on more professional responsibilities. Our pasts, and all the memories they contain, are important reference points for our future. So when the future seems murky, start by asking yourself, *What have I always wanted to do?* Then pay attention to the thoughts that have been hanging around with you for quite some time. There are probably a lot of ideas that you will uncover that you can immediately apply to your current situation.

Please note that we're not advocates of the "just quit your job and change your life" mentality. Rather, we encourage you to get in touch with your own vision and see what tweaks you can make to act more intentionally to achieve your goals.

For many people, dreaming about and pinpointing their career dreams is not easy. This does take conscious work. It will help get you going to start reading more. Try to gain information from a variety of sources — especially ones that you're not drawn to naturally. For example, read magazines completely outside your industry to see what the issues are in other markets. Pull up news websites from other parts of the country or the world — what are they reporting on? And subscribe to newsletters from companies you admire or want to learn more about, even though you may know very little about them. Innovative ideas don't only come from creative types. Innovation involves making connections and connecting the dots to generate new ideas, and anyone can do that. For more ideas and more connections, start connecting more dots.

And then be sure to spend some time writing out your thoughts and ideas. Writing is a clarifying process. A warrior monk we know believes that you don't know anything until you've had a chance to write about it. That's worthwhile advice.

We've found that the most successful Sparks always seek guidance from other successful individuals. So in developing your vision, it's also valuable to seek mentors so you can draw inspiration from the people you respect and admire. Your mentors might offer up some great ideas you should be engaging in to help generate a personal vision. Asking someone to be your mentor doesn't have to feel like a marriage proposal — you don't need to get down on one knee and ask your prospective mentor to walk with you during good times and bad. An easier and less awkward way to approach a prospective mentor is to ask that person out to lunch so you can learn about his or her career. Most people are flattered to share their history with others and discuss the career decisions they've made. And if someone you ask is not interested in meeting with you, don't sweat it — this person probably wasn't going to be a good mentor anyway.

Consider Sean's career transition. The combination of being in a rut as a pilot and overhearing that conversation about Courtney's consulting work was enough to reignite the Spark within him and inspire him to find out more. Sure, he had years of training, discipline, and communication skills, but he was also primed to make the move into a new chapter in his life. And he jumped at it. That's what Sparks do.

Networking is also very beneficial, though just the thought of it makes some people cringe. That's because most of us think of networking as going to a hotel conference room, grabbing a Sharpie, and writing your name on a badge. Sure, there are networking events like this, but if they're not for you, choose something more comfortable, such as simply connecting with people online and asking them questions so you can learn about them and their careers. Just as in your mentoring relationships, an effective networker always does more listening than talking. Casual conversations with success-oriented people can spark many great ideas about what you could be doing in your future if you gave yourself permission to be creative and imaginative.

We've seen networking pay off all the time. Lauren, a friend of ours, is an expert informal networker, and her network inspired a major career change. When she was working as an account manager in a sales organization, she'd find herself talking with professionals from different industries all the time. Her conversations weren't strictly business; she loved hearing people's stories and learning how they found themselves in their role. Through her client interactions, she learned that several of them were going to school part-time to advance their expertise. They were clearly passionate about their career and wanted to develop their knowledge in their field. This made her wonder whether she was passionate about her work. It didn't take her long to conclude that, no, she was not. As she thought more about her interests, she kept coming back to writing. She had already earned her master's degree in fine arts but didn't have the courage to leave behind the security of her job to pursue writing full-time.

As Lauren started imagining more about what she would have to do to take the leap and write full-time, she started talking to individuals who had taken a big risk to pursue their dreams — like her yoga teacher, who founded and managed a yoga co-operative, which was a collection of yoga teachers who offered classes in corporations. "How'd you get this off the ground?" Lauren asked. Her teacher confided that she had sought a supplemental income through teaching to help bring her dream to fruition. This got Lauren thinking: *Maybe I could be a part-time yoga instructor and full-time writer and live in spartan-like conditions until I sell some work.*

After some serious contemplation, Lauren made the commitment to her goal and started to prepare — financially, emotionally, and otherwise — for the first big step she'd have to take to move closer to her professional dream. It took her a few years before she had the confidence, courage, and financial resources to draw up her resignation letter to her employer and start something entirely new. But now she's proud that working as a writer by day and yoga instructor by night has given her the time to live her dream and experience the success that's meaningful to her. (Lauren has since been published in several journals and amassed a following for her work "Short Sweet Poems.")

COURAGE TO ACT

A personal vision is always an important aspect of your Spark development. So is your ability to take action. But sometimes this is difficult because there is real risk involved, and the world doesn't always reward those who make big changes or who try to break the mold. For instance, a common response when a lawyer decides to quit a law firm and become a schoolteacher is, "Why is he doing this? Is he nuts?" When a marketing manager takes a bold, new approach with a client campaign, many stand back and smirk, "Good luck with *that* one!"

We all felt this type of pressure ourselves when we were leaving the military. Our colleagues asked openly on several occasions why we were "quitting." In our minds, we weren't quitting; we had just completed our service commitment and were ready to move on to the next step in our careers. And yes, we know how others' opinions can make you feel insecure as you decide to live more intentionally with your vision. It might even make you question why you're contemplating a new path. But that shouldn't prevent you from taking action. It might just mean you have to establish a new support network to encourage you on your journey.

Beyond feeling societal pressures, we also have to battle ourselves and the routines we've been building. We're creatures of habit, of course, and it's hard to break our habits even when they aren't doing us — or the people around us — any good or taking us to where we want to be. Sometimes our routines are even running us into the ground.

BURNOUT IS VERY REAL

Courtney's Story

Our time is precious, the days of our lives are numbered, and to make the most of the time we have, we need to think hard about how we spend our time, day in and day out.

I always have believed this, but my *appreciation* for this idea somehow became distorted along the way, maybe because I recognized at an early age that our society affirms and rewards hard work. *James worked sixty hours this week — what a stud! Lisa pulled an all-nighter to get the client project done — what a hero! Lydia comes in on Saturdays to get ahead — she's committed.* Working hard is important. But all the time? And without question? There's a workplace reality we all have to face: working hard *all the time* can feel right in the moment — until it doesn't. And the kicker is that burnout sneaks up on you and then hits you like a freight train.

I used to think burnout was for people who just couldn't hack hard work. I know, I know, that sounds cavalier. But when I'd hear my colleagues talk about taking time off or grabbing a much-needed break, I'd listen and enjoy daydreaming with them about how they were going to spend their time away — but I didn't get it. To me, "taking a break" was just an excuse people made to grab some extra vacation days. Who needed a vacation when there was so much more work to be done? I shudder now thinking there was a season of my life when I thought time away from working was purely for slackers.

I'm not sure when exactly my ideas about hard work turned into an obsession, or when my self-identity became tied up so tightly with work, though I'm sure it had something to do with starting Lead Star. I don't think either Angie or I envisioned how consuming our company would be. Add to that the fact that we were *learning* about business while *running* a business, and it's safe to say that every day was filled with challenge, surprise, excitement, and frustration. This happened until we finally got our footing, which was about five years into our business.

Once year five came, Angie and I were beginning to get the hang of things. We knew what we needed to do to run the back office, market our firm, deliver our services, and smooth out our cash flow. And we became quite good at it. So good that we had more business than time to do it. We were traveling to client sites each week, working endless hours on airplanes and hotels, trying to manage our family lives, and hiring more employees to help support the firm. I quickly discovered that my traditional long working hours — 7:00 a.m. to 5:00 p.m. — weren't enough to manage all of my responsibilities. I started getting into the habit of waking up at 5:00 and working twelve straight hours, then spending time with my family before working — again — before bed. This schedule felt necessary, and while I kept telling my husband and myself that it was short-term, days turned into weeks and weeks turned into months. There seemed to be nothing "short-term" about it. This work schedule was becoming my life. And little did I know, but I was backsliding as a Spark.

During this period of intense operations, I was losing touch with Angie, though I didn't realize it, and with Lead Star too. Angie and I just stopped talking to each other. It was nothing intentional — we were just so busy meeting demands. Neither one of us was checking in with the other to see if we were really living the vision we had for our careers and our business. And I was so focused on keeping our firm running that I wasn't doing anything to nurture it. I wasn't leading it . . . I was *reacting* to it. Soon I was resenting it because it felt like it was sucking the life out of me. In truth, it was.

I felt like, looked like, and acted like a zombie. One day, when I was near exhaustion, I walked past a mirror and looked at the person I saw. *Who is* she *and what happened to her?* I started to think it was about sleep — I just needed to get some sleep. But my attempts to get some rest didn't do the trick. Then I thought I needed a vacation. But during my week off with my family — when I was unable to be present with them emotionally — I thought, *No, I really need something more.*

When I got back to work, I sat down at the computer and poured my heart out in a letter to Angie, confessing that I had reached my emotional and physical limits and couldn't go on without taking a break. I have to admit that I felt very weak and full of shame as I stated that I was going to reduce my work hours significantly starting August 1 and that this was going to last until January 1. During these five months, I'd disengage from weekly firm meetings and activities, though I committed to delivering the remaining projects I was responsible for that year. I also committed to generating new business for the following year so that both the team and I could start the new year strong.

I knew that my absence was going to create some frustration and concern with my team, but I also committed to ensuring that I transitioned out of daily operations responsibly. And I worked hard with my team to support my time away (and am forever grateful for how everyone stepped up to ensure that the business ran smoothly without me).

The truth is, when August 1 hit, I still found it difficult to pull back, to actually allow myself the space away from work I had so carefully planned. Slowly I began to develop a new routine — a nonroutine! — that allowed me to return to my vision for my life. I started exercising again, spending focused time with my family, and working on more strategic aspects of the firm so I could fall back in love with it. I also reengaged my network, an effort that allowed me to shape business deals that ended up being very valuable — and quite scalable — for the firm.

What was most surprising was how much more successful I was — as a wife, parent, and professional — after I'd imposed this time off in my life and reset my routine. I had never realized that in order to accelerate your success you first need to slow down deliberately so as to gain clarity around what is truly the best use of your time and talents.

That fall taught me some of the most valuable lessons I've learned as a professional and as a leader. As humans, we all have maximum capacities — even Sparks. We are not machines. If we pay true attention to how we feel about the way we are working and take the time to determine whether this is the productive approach for us, we end up being better. My old habit of just continuing to do more and more has been replaced by respecting that success breeds stress. Relaxing and stepping back are not weak actions; they are examples of the often counterintuitive strength you need to measure up personally and professionally. After several months of a reduced schedule, not only was I ready to engage fully, but I was now invigorated because I had overcome a barrier that was limiting my ability to live intentionally.

So yes, burnout is real. And it's certain to keep you too from living your vision for yourself. On your Spark journey, you need to pay attention to the signs, which usually start with taking on more responsibility without modifying your schedule to accommodate it. This is difficult to do, because we like to say, "Yes! I can do more!" or, "Yes, I can volunteer for this committee," or, "Yes, I can work on Saturdays." And our yeses tend to get us pretty far in life. But eventually this strategy will get us to a plateau, which is when the only word that'll get us any further is "no."

Everyone hates saying no, which is just an admission that we have either limits or boundaries. But "no" can also be a secret weapon for a Spark. I should have said no when I realized that my intense work pace wasn't a life strategy for success. And I'm confident that, had I paused before my burnout hit and asked, *Are all the things I'm doing really necessary? Is everything — my family, my business relationships, my business — okay? Is this the life I envisioned for myself?* I would have realized there were changes I could make to get back on track.

I've since spent a lot of time working with ambitious professionals on learning to say no. I start by trying to help them understand their priorities, their vision, and what they should start doing — and stop doing — to act intentionally in their lives and to make decisions that matter. I can attest that when you say no just once, you will be one step closer to saying it again. Before you know it, you'll break out of a routine that could be bringing you to your knees and be ready to start a new pattern: not only will your performance level increase, but you will have a newfound capacity that allows you to move closer to your goals.

MAKE THE COMMITMENT

All progress begins with a decision, which is followed by action. Or as one of our clients says, whatever you do, "do it on purpose."

As a vice president at Boston Scientific, Allen Meacham challenges his sales organization to live their lives on purpose. He tells them, "Whatever you do, mean to do it, live your life on purpose" — whether that's consulting with patients, educating physicians on new products, or even taking a break. Allen illustrates the last point by saying that if he's going to spend time with his family watching football, he's going to be fully committed to it. The same goes for giving speeches or putting together sales conferences. He's found that when you do things *on purpose*, you get the most joy and benefit out of the experience, because you're giving it your full attention and presence. He often shares with his team, "If you're going to work twenty hours one day, then mean to do it, and if you're going to take the day off, be off. If you live on purpose, you will be your best and you won't look back on your life with personal or professional regrets."

This same level of commitment is essential for you to make the progress you'd like to see in your own life. You've probably witnessed some failures when people, teams, or organizations say they're going to do something but don't *really* commit to it — like diets, exercise routines, educational pursuits, job changes, sales campaigns, projects, and new business initiatives. In fact, think of all the money, time, and effort wasted when businesses invest in new technology no one chooses to adopt or create corporate policies no one cares to uphold.

Think about yourself. Consider all the energy you may have spent, emotional and otherwise, on making decisions but not following them up with real effort. If you want to experience the change you envision for yourself, it's critical that you create the context that will allow you to succeed.

PLANNING FOR CHANGE

Angie's Story

The Marine Corps has many sayings and "-isms" that offer great life lessons. One of my favorites is: "A plan is a reference point for change." As you develop your vision and bolster your commitment to act, it's important to think about creating a draft plan regarding your next steps forward. Without a draft, you'll flounder. That's not to say that you'll fail, but the harsh reality is that you're not confronting your future with as much focus as you should. Without a plan, you can find yourself quickly feeling scattered.

I felt this way when I welcomed my first son, Judge, into the world. I had a hard time figuring out if I was a "working mom" or a "mom working" — I struggled with balancing these two roles and had trouble deciding when to be what.

So I attempted to blend these roles by not putting any sort of structure in place to focus on. Since I had a home office, I reasoned, I could work when the baby slept during the day and then again in the evenings when he was in bed. I could also work on weekends, when my husband Matt, an active-duty Marine, was home from work to watch our son. And of course, when my son was awake during the day, my laptop was always within arm's reach so I could maintain updates on work. When I traveled to client sites, either Matt would take vacation days to stay with Judge or I'd pack up the baby and gear, head to the airport, and meet my mom or another family member at my destination so they could watch Judge while I worked.

As a mom, I wanted to lead a lifestyle company. But as a business owner, like Courtney, I wanted to grow our firm. Of course, these two ideas were in conflict with each other, and in truth, I never put any real effort into resolving them. So I hovered between both roles — mom *and* business owner — without committing fully to either one. As a result, I became a distracted mom and business owner, and I wasn't succeeding to the best of my ability in either role. (I'm not even going to mention how I was doing in the wife role. I'm just blessed to have an understanding husband.)

But as luck would have it, since I couldn't strike a balance on my own, a major life event forced my hand. At the time, my family and I were living in base housing on Marine Corps Base Quantico while Matt commuted to and from the Pentagon, where he worked. One night when he came home he made an important and significant announcement: he'd had the job offer of a lifetime — unfortunately, the job was located in Iraq and he'd be spending the entire year there.

I was shocked (to say the least). This possibility wasn't even on my radar. We had just moved into our house, and Matt had been at his current assignment for less than one year. He was supposed to be nondeployable for three years. And he had just recently spent time in Iraq and Africa, so I mistakenly presumed that he had done his time overseas, that he'd punched his ticket and we wouldn't have to deal with his absence for several more years. But now this? *An entire year* when we had an eighteen-month-old? *During the surge period in the Iraq war?* It was just way too much. And it wasn't like we could argue with the Marine Corps, which doesn't really negotiate job offers or offer you the professional courtesy of a heads-up.

I spent several long days contemplating scenarios of how I was going to prepare myself and Judge emotionally for Matt's absence, all the while also trying to figure out how I was going to manage all the responsibilities already in front of me: single-parenting for a year, running a business, running a household, etc. And the first conclusion I came to was that I couldn't do it alone. I decided to move back to Michigan to live near my parents so they could help with Judge while I traveled. I also knew that as Judge approached two and started to resist naps, my past work arrangement wasn't going to work in the future. (And to be honest, it really wasn't working to begin with.) So I found a wonderful day care where he could spend his days. Our small home in Michigan lacked a home office, so I started to arrange a separate workspace; what I found wasn't as spacious or aesthetically inspiring as any I'd had before, but it was functional and would have to do.

In just a matter of days, I had achieved something that I hadn't in the previous eighteen months: a plan. After a very emotional and tearful good-bye to Matt, Judge and I made our move and settled into our new life. I quickly discovered something very surprising, considering the circumstances: I was relieved. By making a conscious effort to structure my work and life, I suddenly had the ability to focus on all the roles I filled. Whatever maternal guilt I experienced by shuffling my son off to day care was replaced by the satisfaction I felt when I could be present with him whenever we were together. As my harried life became much smoother I found a newfound confidence in all the roles I had juggled before. What's more, I was experiencing success at a higher level because I wasn't chasing the multitasking myth — the false notion that I could do several things at once with the same level of excellence as I could bring to any one of those things.

The year apart from my husband wasn't easy, but it was a great year of personal discovery. I learned the value of committing myself to my decisions and of creating a lifestyle to support my choices. Like anyone else, I'm not always going to be great at applying these ideas. But I am now careful about taking on commitments, because I want to experience success and gratification in whatever I do. In short, I always try to think ahead about what new commitments will mean for me and my daily schedule before taking them on.

I know I'm not the only one who struggles with committing fully to personal decisions by creating the necessary structure to transition toward a better life. I've seen this struggle among friends, colleagues, and clients — aspiring entrepreneurs who have great business plans but don't shop them around for investors, for instance, or those who want to be promoted to the next level of responsibility but never spend the time gathering the experiences — like networking and further education — to make themselves better candidates.

Of course, there are always going to be the twists and turns that are a natural part of life. Some of those twists can stall you from acting intentionally on the decisions that are most important to you. But as long as you don't create roadblocks for yourself, you'll be well on your way to being one of those Sparks who shape their own future so they can lead their life on their own terms.

SPARK ACTIONS

To honor your future self by making decisions that are aligned with your values:

- Reconcile the disconnect between where you are now and where you want to be.
- Commit yourself to growth and seek out challenges that help you evolve as a Spark.
- Create a plan for the changes you seek so you can commit fully to your goals.
- Recognize that there are limits to your capacity — to prevent burnout you have to say no many times to leave room for a few valuable yeses.

CHARGING AHEAD

This chapter is all about you — your vision for yourself, ideas on how to develop your vision, and ways to avoid those activities that prevent you from acting with intent. The following resources on www.sparkslead.us are designed to help you understand what you can start doing today to honor your vision with effort and action.

- *Your Vision:* This visioning exercise will help you explore your goals for yourself — both short-term and long-term — and the small actions you can take today to start accomplishing them.
- *Burnout:* The pace we keep up can unintentionally derail us from achieving the success we seek. Do you feel like you're near burnout? Take the quiz and see what you can do to get your life — and career — back on track. (Also share the quiz with your colleagues — it can be very helpful to get the team view as it relates to burnout.) We also offer several actions you can take to curb burnout immediately.
- *Action Plan:* When was the last time you created a plan that will help you focus, personally and professionally, on what you need to do to build the habits that will help you make daily decisions that matter most? This action plan will help you look at your next 100 days and prompt you to identify very specific actions you can take that will lead you toward your vision.

Once you're through reflecting on the intentional actions you can take that will help you develop as a Spark, you'll be ready to move on to the next chapter and learn how to serve others so they can be Sparks too. When leaders step up and bring service to the teams they are a part of, the impact on the level of camaraderie these teams experience is transformative.

6

BE OF SERVICE: RECOGNIZE AND MEET OTHERS' NEEDS

Sparks are always aware of others' needs and take action to meet them. This outward focus strengthens relationships and creates camaraderie and connection.

WE HUMANS CRAVE COMMUNITY, which is a good thing considering that in today's knowledge economy, no matter who you are or where you work, you have to work with — and through — people. Whether it's cross-functional teams, colleagues from different geographies, or special projects groups, we're constantly being paired with others and challenged to collaborate and produce great results. This can be easy *or* it can be difficult, depending on the group you're part of and its willingness to behave like a team. But Sparks understand that in order to get the most out of their teams, *they* need to serve — and to show others how to serve as well.

Building a team can be difficult because everything depends, of course, on the people who make up the team — we're all so different. Our life experiences vary greatly, we have competing needs and priorities, and our agendas are often misaligned, all of which can complicate the team-building process and make our desire for community feel out of reach. But this doesn't mean that teamwork isn't achievable. In fact, many of us have had great experiences on teams that made us feel valued, appreciated, and respected. We've also had some frustrating team experiences, where the dynamic isn't in sync and people seemingly can't come together effectively.

So what makes the difference between teams that are easy and those that are difficult? The presence — or more precisely, the absence — of service-based leadership. Sparks lead through service.

Service-based leadership is a concept seldom taught and rarely talked about outside of the military, but it was integral to our success both during and after our time in uniform. At its core, service is selflessly acting on behalf of others to ensure their success. Service is the essence of an unselfish act. And when you act selflessly, you can be the Spark who transforms a group of individuals into a team.

Service can be demonstrated in the simplest ways. For example, as officers, we were instructed to always eat last, ensuring that others had food before we filled our plates. This act communicated that we emphasized our team's needs before our own. We were also advised to deliver "hip-pocket classes" — that is, to be ready at a moment's notice to teach and train our teams whenever they were experiencing downtime so that we were always learning and developing together. This act reinforced that our role was to ensure that we were bettering each other and growing together. And service was represented in one of our sayings, "Mission first, people always," which makes it clear that results and people are both critical priorities.

Service in your world might look like checking in and seeing how your colleagues are doing, or giving someone your undivided attention, or taking the initiative to finish up a mundane task that no one is eager to do.

Here's the point: when people feel cared for because you're serving them, they begin to feel safe and experience your commitment to them. They're also able to focus less on themselves and more on their team and the results they're seeking to deliver. So when one Spark chooses to serve, the benefits can be unlimited.

Service is one of the counterinstinctual behaviors — we're not born with service-based motivations. On the contrary, we're born pretty selfish. Children and most teenagers don't wake up thinking *How can I help Mom today?* Service is even countercultural. Our Western society reinforces total self-focus in the messages that bombard us every day — "Have it your way." "Look out for number one." "Because you're worth it."

With development, support, and context cues, we can shift our focus from self to others, but doing so doesn't erase the instinct — it's still there. Yet with the right level of awareness and discipline, it can be managed. When you're able to demonstrate service to others, you quickly learn that the benefits of the team experience far exceed any of the great results you can achieve on your own. That's when you're acting like a Spark.

Like all Spark behaviors, service is a deliberate choice you make. When you choose to serve, you might not realize immediately how your efforts connect to someone else's success, but rest assured — they do.

"COCA-COLA"

Angie's Story

The Marine Corps is an interesting group. I have no scientific data to support this claim, but I believe there is no other organization in the world that has more members tattooed with its logo than the United States Marine Corps. Why do they do that? Sure, alcohol might be a contributing factor, but it's not the motivator. What motivates Marines to get Corps tattoos is their lifelong pride in the organization and commitment to it. This pride and commitment aren't achieved by random chance. They stem from the Corps' focus on "service before self" — a mindset introduced on day one when you sign up to be a Marine.

I'd like to think that when I earned my commission as a second lieutenant I was already a service-based leader, but that's just not entirely true. I was twenty-one and still pretty self-focused. I may have learned about service-based leadership during my instruction and come to understand it conceptually, but I didn't truly demonstrate it until after I had experienced it. That happened at TBS (The Basic School) — that six-month school I mentioned earlier where I was struggling to learn everything Marine Corps green.

What I didn't mention previously was how challenging some of our instructors were and how they added to the TBS dynamic — let me tell you, they were tough. First, many were physically intimidating — not only did these guys eat their Wheaties, but they hit the gym every day with an intensity unknown to mankind. And there were others who were just aggressive. I once got a black eye and bloody nose when I was paired up with our instructor during knife-fighting drills. (There was no taking it easy on this five-foot-three Marine.)

But as strong and fierce as all these guys were, they were no match for Captain Harper, possibly the loudest — and proudest — Marine in the Corps. To reinforce his image, he didn't want us to call him by his rank and surname. *Oh no.* He made it clear that we were to call him "Coca-Cola" because, the way he saw it, he was the "real thing."

And there was no doubt about it — he was the real thing. Coca-Cola might have been five-foot-five, but I don't think anyone had ever told him that, because he walked around like he was seven feet tall. He was my company's executive officer, and it was his number-one priority to ensure that everyone who graduated from *his* school, to serve in *his* Corps, was going to be pushed, challenged, and scrutinized until they rose to his superior level of performance. Those who didn't (or couldn't), he reminded us, could take a bus ride back home back to our mamas.

Well, I'm no dummy. I took Coca-Cola's threats seriously. I also knew that, with all of my struggles, it'd be a good strategy to fly below Coca-Cola's radar. I had seen him "counsel" my colleagues on their performance. I didn't want that additional heat brought my way, so I did what any good Marine would do: used camouflage to my advantage. When we were in the field doing training, I did my best to blend into the woods when he was around. In a classroom environment, I would sit behind my tall colleagues so he wouldn't see me.

I thought I was doing a pretty good job of escaping his attention until one day, when I was sitting in class with 200 of my colleagues, our instructor had a note passed to him by an admin. He opened the note, read it, pointed directly to me, and said, "Lieutenant, you need to go see Captain Harper."

In that instant I felt like I had just been punched in the gut. *What had I done?* I can remember the real sense of trepidation I had as I walked to his office. When I arrived, I knocked on his door and announced that I was reporting as ordered. Once granted permission to enter his office, I walked smartly to his desk, stood at attention, and mentally prepared myself for whatever was to come my way.

But Coca-Cola's next move surprised me. "Sit down," he instructed firmly. As soon as I did, he moved from behind his desk to a chair right next to me and leaned in, in preparation for what he was about to say next.

"Angie," he said in a tone I had never heard before — it sounded strangely like compassion. Instantly I thought, *Oh dear God, this is when I find out that I'm just not making the cut.* But then he continued: "I've got some really sad news for you. I just got off the phone with your mom — your grandmother has passed away."

He then paused, giving me time to process the news. As soon as he saw tears filling up my eyes, he asked gently, "What can I do to get you with your family right now?"

Before I could even formulate a response to Coca-Cola's question, he started sharing what he had already done. "So far, I have a colleague waiting outside the door to take you to your apartment so you can pack. He'll drive you to Reagan National so you can pick up a ticket at the counter that I've reserved for you. I called your parents — they know when you're arriving and will meet you at the airport. I talked to the training officer — he knows you'll be gone but is prepared to give you some one-on-one attention when you return so you can catch up. Angie, *what else can we do to help you out?*"

All I could think was, *Else? What else?* He had already done so much. In my moment of need, he was responding better than any friend would have. And what's more, he wasn't done.

"Angie, I know that once you get home you're going to start feeling like you're missing out on a lot of instruction and you should get back to training. But please, take your time at home — be with your family. The Marine Corps is very interesting — we've existed for 222 years *without you*. We can last a week more. You can offer your parents some comfort by your presence. Just go home and stay home and come back when you're ready."

And just like that, despite my grief, I felt such a complete sense of relief and comfort because I knew I was being taken care of — and that Coca-Cola was working all sorts of magic behind the scenes so my family and I could be together.

When I finally made it home, not only was it good to be home, but what made it especially memorable was hearing a knock on my parents' door within minutes of arriving and opening it to discover a flower delivery man carrying the largest bouquet of flowers I had ever seen in my whole life. I opened the card, and, of course, it was signed by Coca-Cola and my entire TBS class. I was so moved that even from afar, I was being cared for, and I was so proud I was working for an organization that looked out for me. My loyalty to the organization increased tenfold that day.

I've reflected upon this experience quite a bit since then because it was such an important leadership lesson for me as a Spark. Coca-Cola taught me that to be a leader you can be tough, you can be aggressive, you can have demanding standards — but if you *can't* be compassionate, empathetic, and caring, you're never going to build a team of people who feel valued and connected.

You can imagine that after I returned to training I paid much closer attention to Coca-Cola — he had made quite an impression on me. What I observed was that, sure, he had been an exceptional leader in my time of need, but service wasn't just a onetime event for him. He was *always* serving — it just looked different based on the circumstances. For example, why was he so exacting about standards? He was training us for combat so we could be our best when faced with overwhelming circumstances. Why was I always hiding from him? He was always there! He cared enough about us to be present.

I learned from Coca-Cola that service, true service, is meeting people's needs so they can be their best. And sometimes service can be demonstrated in the smallest ways. Think of Coca-Cola — he may have spent only thirty minutes organizing all of the resources to get me home to be with my family, but think of what that thirty-minute time investment produced: my lifelong loyalty *and* commitment.

I never did end up getting that tattoo to showcase my pride in the Marines, but let's just say I have enough stickers and sweat-shirts that convey my Semper Fi spirit.

WHAT SERVICE LOOKS LIKE

If service is about meeting people's needs, it's important to know that we all have needs and they differ from person to person. To serve others you first need to understand the basic kinds of human needs.

There's been a lot of research conducted on basic human needs, and Dr. Abraham Maslow's is the most groundbreaking and famous. During the 1940s, he published a paper on the hierarchy of human needs, which were later organized into a pyramid: physiological needs, safety, love and belonging, esteem, and self-actualization. Self-actualization — the stage where you focus on your growth and development — is the goal for all humans, according to humanistic psychology. To reach self-actualization, however, you have to fulfill your most basic needs first.

As humans, it's important to know that our needs are never static — they change with each stage and circumstance of life we find ourselves in. They can even change hour by hour, which is easy to conceptualize. For example, if you've ever been hungry in a meeting or lost and confused while traveling in a foreign country, your focus isn't on your esteem. Your focus is on fulfilling basic physiological and security needs, respectively; once those needs are met, you can move on to higher-order needs. Or consider a major life event. If you have ever been laid off from a job or taken care of an ailing parent, you know that during such a time your primary focus isn't on career fulfillment or mastery of a hobby. It's not that these ideas are excluded from your thought process, but that they feel distant because they aren't pressing.

The Maslow pyramid will be helpful to reference as you look to grow in your career and your life. In fact, the chart might even give you some insight into what's holding you back from being the Spark you're capable of becoming. Where are you on that pyramid?

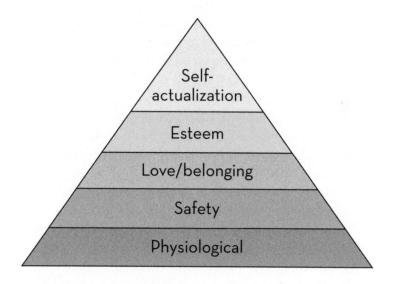

Maslow's pyramid is also exceptionally useful for you as a Spark striving to be a service-based leader, because it's important to understand that the people around you — your friends, family members, colleagues, and even your boss — have personal, unique needs located somewhere on that pyramid. To be of service to those around you, you have to first figure out what these needs are and how you can personally help them fulfill those needs.

Acts of service don't have to be flashy, fancy, or expensive. They can be as easy as referring your friend's newly formed business to your neighbor or helping a colleague prepare for a promotion interview. Service can be as simple as active listening, which is a very rare commodity in our hurried worlds. After all, you've probably experienced "drive-by leadership before" — people passing you and saying, "Howya doin'?" but not sticking around for the reply. To be a Spark and cultivate influence with others, do what others don't — *stop and actively listen.*

It's rewarding to serve others and to help them reach their potential. It actually makes us happy. In numerous studies, MRI scans have shown that acts of giving activate the craving and pleasure reward area in our brain; incidentally, it is the same area that is delighted when we eat chocolate. In other words, giving makes us feel good. And our happiness is important — not just because of the immediate joy we experience personally, but because happiness is linked to success in many different life outcomes, like improved health, positive relationships, career success, and goal attainment.

When individuals commit to service, it's not too long before they spark positive service behavior from others around them. And beyond the intrinsic value of helping others, this ripple effect can often be used to address pressing business challenges.

While working with Schlumberger, a global oil field services company and long-standing Lead Star client, we learned that one segment was experiencing an increased number of safety incidents among its newly hired employees. One of the company's executives, Mark O'Byrne, believed that if these newer employees could just get additional mentoring from the more tenured professionals on what to do or not do while on the job, they would engage in better safety practices and have a more positive overall experience on the job site.

We started working with Mark to develop a mentoring program in which we would train prospective mentors on how to be of service to their mentees — those newly hired employees. The mentors weren't necessarily managers or supervisors, but they were definitely Sparks — people who saw themselves as offering a real solution to an organizational challenge. The mentors volunteered to receive training and to take on additional opportunities to help newer employees better acclimate to their roles.

In our training, we gave them an idea of what service in their mentor-mentee relationship would look like:

- Introducing themselves to their newly assigned mentee and spending time asking open-ended questions so they could better understand their mentee's background
- Helping their mentee acquire the safety gear needed to do the job and then following up to make sure the mentee had the gear or helping the mentee deal with any problems in acquiring the gear
- When possible, working alongside their mentee to observe his or her processes (and coaching when appropriate)
- Including their mentee in meals and breaks so that their mentee never felt left alone
- Always inviting their mentee to informal gatherings so the mentee could meet fellow employees
- Providing positive encouragement and going out of their way to say something to their mentee about a job well done
- Helping their mentee understand the unwritten rules of the corporate culture
- Explaining acronyms, expressions, and lingo the mentee might not have heard before

Simple stuff, right? But sometimes the simplest stuff gets lost in the shuffle, especially if it's not communicated directly. As we rolled out the mentoring program at Schlumberger, we heard quickly from many mentors about how helpful it was to spell out actions they could take on behalf of new hires. We also heard from mentees, who shared how much they appreciated having a mentor, someone with whom they could ask "stupid questions," and how they benefited from knowing that someone was always looking out for them. We also heard from Mark, who was excited to observe a positive cultural shift as mentors became intent on developing new hires and setting them up for long-term safety *and* career success.

SHIFTING YOUR PERSPECTIVE FOR A STRONGER TEAM

Sometimes service is the essential key for helping you navigate difficult relationships. For example, you might be experiencing a tenuous client relationship. Service-based leadership might help you think about what you're *not doing* to help make this relationship work. Or maybe you're in constant conflict with a colleague. Just think of how your relationship could advance when you think about your colleague's needs in the relationship, not just yours. Or you and your boss might not see eye to eye. Maybe you've never considered your boss and his or her family situation; perhaps there's difficulty at home with the spouse, or maybe your boss has been under a lot of pressure from higher-ups. When you consider other people's perspective from *their* view, you develop empathy for them, which can inspire you to be more thoughtful in your interactions.

Your service efforts are limited only by your imagination and willingness to take initiative. As you think about how to enact service in your environment, a good place to start is by thinking about the people you're connected to day in and day out and asking yourself some questions about them. You probably know some of the answers, but maybe not all of them:

- What is their background?
- Why did they choose this career or employer?
- What is their family situation?
- What are their interests?
- What makes them happy? What makes them tick?
- How can I add value to this relationship?

That last question is sometimes difficult to figure out. We often undervalue the type of service we can offer to others, or think it's not our place to offer it. And it might feel weird thinking you can serve someone who is older or has more experience than you. How do you do this without being awkward? For starters, Sparks are sincere with their intentions. If you think you can add value for someone, ensure that your *motive* is to help that person and that your *focus* is on empowering him or her. That last piece is key.

It's important to know that true service isn't about coddling or enabling — it's about empowering. Coddling is pampering or babying people, offering them insincere compliments and not giving them the honest feedback they need to hear. Enabling is either doing the job for someone or lowering the standard so that person can meet it. All of this is detrimental to you and to the other person because an enabled person never becomes fully independent of you.

Empowering entails providing resources, giving information, and helping others become more successful. For example, we've met countless executives who'd be lost without their assistants. Their service efforts — from effective planning and gatekeeping to bookmarking articles on relevant subjects — ensure smooth operations and allow the executives they work for to stay informed and focused. We've also met many junior employees who stand out in the crowd just by the way they communicate:

they provide information that has real meaning to the receiver, not just to the sender. We've also seen peers serve each other by offering difficult feedback because they care enough *not* to sweep uncomfortable issues under the rug.

Service to others is a habit. To start building it you need to recognize that there are some common workplace barriers that prevent us from demonstrating service. But with the right strategies in place, those barriers won't stop you from being a Spark who can unite your team through leadership.

WHAT CAN WE DO TOGETHER THAT WE CAN'T DO ALONE?

Courtney's Story

I've been fortunate to work on some pretty amazing teams where leadership was present consistently. You've probably experienced this too. *Some teams just feel better than others.* Looking back on my career, the great (and not so great) teams stand out, because even today I can recall how I felt when I was a part of them. On the great ones, I felt like my colleagues cared about me, my boss respected my initiative, and my daily actions connected to the organization's success.

Early on in my career, I had the fantastic opportunity to work at Rational Software as a sales manager — my first professional experience post–Marine Corps. It was invigorating to work with a team that rewarded hard work and results. From our bosses to our support staff, there was a strong sense of camaraderie that came across in the actions that people took on each other's behalf. I can remember one situation where my boss, Mark, came up to me with a movie ticket to an afternoon show and said, "Courtney, your commitment is amazing, but there's also a time to relax. Get out of the office this afternoon." I was impressed that he not only knew I loved going to the movies but also anticipated that I was feeling stressed. I felt relieved that he gave me permission to unwind on a workday. I also think about our sales coordinator, Linda, and our administrative assistant, Jeanette. They both paid close attention to what was going on in the business and ensured that my team and I were never without the resources we needed to do our jobs. Our company achieved tremendous success and was eventually acquired by IBM. I like to think that the culture, not just the product and the results, made it an even more attractive acquisition.

But I've also worked in environments where the *lack* of leadership at all levels was notable. On those teams that were less-than-best, I often felt frustrated, angry, and anxious. On those teams, team members bickered constantly, bosses were inconsistent, and we all had our guard up because we never knew when we were going to get stabbed in the back. Some people call teams like these "toxic environments," while others call them unhealthy. I'm reminded of my time in the Marines when we'd say, "One sick ship would sink the fleet." There's only one remedy for these environments: service-based leadership.

Then there was the time I worked briefly at a large law firm. I can easily recall how the absence of service-based leadership there resonated with me. Each day I felt isolated, disconnected, and more like a commodity than a person. Although my colleagues were brilliant, many of them had not had the opportunity to learn behavior-based leadership. At this firm, leadership was all about perceived power, prestige, rank, and authority. If you were senior in title, you were the leader. And that seemed to mean you had a license to act any way you liked — from humiliating others with a screaming outburst to gossiping like a kid in the school yard — and everyone else just had to deal with it.

I was fortunate to never be on the receiving end of the angry outbursts of senior partners, but I saw many associates emotionally withdraw and eventually leave as a result of this frustrating culture. The law firm's management assumed that the young lawyers left because they couldn't hack the long hours, but that was rarely the reason they departed. Most exits had to do with how it felt to work with professionals who didn't understand the value of leadership behavior. It was sad to see so many young, ambitious, and talented lawyers go — and some even leave the profession. In my view, these Sparks (and would-be Sparks) would've flourished if they had experienced service-based leadership.

As a consultant, I've also observed a wide spectrum of service-based leadership in a variety of client environments. Because I work in such a broad cross-section of industries and verticals, my clients enjoy asking me about other clients. When they ask me, "Who are your best clients?" I share that while I try not to have favorites, some certainly stand out. For example, when we worked with Orkin, the pest management company, I once joked with my husband that I was tempted to moonlight at Orkin just so I could get the opportunity to work in a great family-oriented environment. Pest management isn't sexy, but Orkin's corporate culture is most impressive. In fact, Orkin has one of the strongest service-based leadership cultures I've seen. It's clearly an important component of the company, and the leadership works hard to embrace it.

Ziegenfelder is another client that comes to mind — this family-owned company has been manufacturing frozen desserts for three generations, and the strong sense of service to each other is palpable when you're on the plant floor. People care, and that concern for each other translates into a workforce and a management team who continuously go above and beyond to get the job done . . . even when they perform their jobs in ice-cold freezers.

The truth is, I'd work nearly anywhere that has strong leadership. In fact, I think we all would, mostly because we've all had personal experiences where a lack of leadership made us want to quit our job (or we *did* quit our job). The emotions connected to these experiences may range greatly, but the common denominator is an absence of leadership. In other words, people don't quit their jobs — they quit the people with whom they work.

But to be fair, let's allow these organizations to get off the hot seat for a second. It's not like they are bad companies full of bad people who want to create a miserable working environment. It's just that they have some of the common barriers that prevent individuals from demonstrating service-based leadership.

The most obvious is *awareness*. Most people just don't know about service-based leadership. And some people feel that it's too simple to be effective. It's as if professionals think that simple service-based leadership practices like listening actively, demonstrating empathy, taking time to get to know the personal stories of the people you work with, and truly seeking to understand how you can add value for someone else are just not that important — not in the face of running a business. It's far too easy to simply dismiss service as something for someone else to do — "That's HR's job."

The second is *pace*. It does take extra discipline and focus to make time for other people in the midst of your busy and hectic schedule. We all want to get everything off our desks before we head out the door at the end of the day. Yet in this quest to get it all done, we sometimes forget to ask ourselves: are we doing what matters for this company and for our teams?

People need to matter, especially in a fast-paced environment. By holding ourselves accountable for practicing service-based leadership, we prevent ourselves from buying into the excuse that we would definitely take the time to lead, but we're just too busy.

Then there's also *unhealthy competition,* which often shows up in unexpected ways on the projects I work on. One noteworthy example is from a retreat I facilitated for the owners of a thriving small business. Our goal in the retreat was to focus on developing their strategy in the face of a rapidly changing industry. But every time we started talking about the organization, it seemed we would end up discussing compensation. After a while I started noticing some snarky attitudes over compensation, as if people felt there wasn't equity or fairness — even after the team had made a tremendous effort to formulate a complex compensation structure that ensured that everyone was paid for the hours they worked, the types of services they performed, and the revenue they brought into the organization. I realized that we couldn't progress to discuss the organization until we resolved this compensation issue, so I asked to see sample monthly earnings reports. That is where things started to get very interesting.

Each owner was earning more than $200,000 *a month* in salary and no owner was out-earning another by more than $10,000. Let me stop right here and acknowledge that, yes, those are some pretty big paychecks. Astronomical, you might say. But the amount wasn't what captured my attention. It was how each owner's earnings were actually pretty similar each month. When everyone agreed that the entire team was contributing comparably to the organization, I had to raise the question: "What exactly is the problem again?"

From my perspective it was clear: they were battling each other each month for the "Top Dog Award," trying to see who could get the highest paycheck. What they were missing was the opportunity to work together, drive higher revenues through collaboration, and spend more time focusing on the pressing areas where their leadership really was needed. In other words, they weren't leading their organization, a point I made clear to them. (One of the joys of consulting is that you get the opportunity to speak truth to power; in fact, candor is often what our clients value most.)

I encouraged the owners to make sure their performance standards and metrics made sense. We had an engaging debate about what was more valuable — a sense of team and a positive culture or a monthly cage match where $10,000 bought you bragging rights but killed the team culture. One by one they agreed that the value of teamwork was priceless. (I guess $10,000 is not a big deal when you are earning $200,000-plus.) Over time, as they all agreed to stop complicating compensation and split their wages evenly, performance improved even more and their conflict dissolved. Coming to understand how they could bring a sense of service to their fellow owners was extremely rewarding for them, both emotionally and financially, as they worked together to position their company for sale.

It's easy for us as humans to be focused on getting our share. It is as if we instinctively seek the biggest piece of the pie, thinking that's all that's available — that the size of the pie is fixed. Yet when we expand our mindset and become service-based leaders, we don't often worry about getting the biggest slice. We actually find ourselves in a position to collaborate more effectively, working with and through others to achieve bigger successes than we initially imagined. We effectively help grow the pie, making sure the team wins. And not surprisingly, when others win, we win too.

Service isn't always easy — there's no magic wand that makes it happen on its own. It takes a lot of personal discipline to put other people's needs first and to think about what you can do to set everyone else up for success. But our challenge to you is simple: take a risk and try it. Give yourself permission to create your own leadership laboratory by purposefully serving for at least ten minutes a day for one solid week. Make an appointment in your Outlook calendar or your cell phone to remind you if you have to. And then just do it. You'll be surprised as you observe your little efforts starting to add up. We promise you that the results you see will give you the motivation to continue the habit.

SOME IMPORTANT SERVICE RULES

As you start thinking about your service-based efforts, there are a few important things to consider before you act on someone else's behalf.

First, to really be a Spark who serves others, anticipate the needs of those around you. Like Coca-Cola, don't make people ask for help — just help them when you see you have the opportunity and resources to do so. When you see someone struggling, take the initiative to approach that person yourself, instead of expecting it to happen the other way around.

When we worked with a financial services firm, one of the advisers shared that when her husband passed away and she found herself single-parenting two young daughters, one of the greatest gifts her team at work gave her was just doing little things consistently without her having to say, "You know, I'm struggling right now and could really use a little help here." As a result, her already strong loyalty to the firm increased tenfold.

When the day care plans of one of our clients fell through on a day he had to present to the CEO, he brought his daughter to work and his colleagues stepped up to entertain the "new employee" while he delivered a focused brief. He later shared that this unexpected level of support not only surprised him but made him brag to his wife about his exceptional workplace.

A colleague of ours observed that his boss was exceptionally busy one week, so he approached her and asked if there was anything she needed help with. "I have this huge presentation to deliver at the end of the week," she said, "and I need a simple template to use for my client. Do you mind? It might take you ten minutes, but it would take me an hour — and I just don't have that kind of time right now!" Our colleague took the initiative to ask for more details about the presentation, and then, rather than giving her a simple template, he spent time researching images that connected to key points in her message. He spent a few hours preparing the PowerPoint deck for her, and when she received it she was overwhelmed by its professional polish and visual impact. As you can imagine, through his ability to offer support to his boss and deliver above and beyond expectations, he firmly secured his position as her go-to guy forevermore.

These are all examples of the little efforts you can make on behalf of others that can really influence how they feel about you, the team they are a part of, and the overall quality of their work experience. But there's another important point about service: when you're serving, do so without any expectation of return. Otherwise stated, *don't keep score.* Sparks influence and inspire best when the service they offer is for the betterment of others.

To be of true service is to give. That's it. Let the reward be that you made someone's life a little easier, a little more enjoyable, and a little more fulfilling. When you remove the quid pro quo from service, you create an environment that motivates people to act because they *want* to, not because they *have* to. This type of service also feels much more sincere to the receiver. No one likes a gift with strings attached.

Finally, to serve — really serve — do it across the board. It's natural to want to serve others who are most like ourselves and with whom we have a natural rapport. But Sparks understand that providing service to some but not all creates an environment conducive to favoritism. As a leader, always look to create environments where everyone, not just a select few, feels valued, appreciated, and connected. When you do, you'll be amazed by the level and spirit of cooperation that can be achieved.

SERVICE IN THE FRIENDLY SKIES

Sean's Story

Whenever I tell people I still fly commercial airplanes for Delta Airlines, they share with me immediately their travel nightmare stories, which typically involve reroutes, sick passengers, lost luggage, or extensive delays. I get it — we all have our travel horror stories.

And don't think we pilots don't know what's going on in the cabin as these horrors unfold. When passengers are experiencing travel inconveniences, we're usually well aware of them and trying to help solve the problems we can. The good news is that this is pretty easy because most routine problems can be addressed by a quick phone call. For example, when we have mechanical challenges, we call maintenance. When we have supply shortages, we call catering. And when we have irate passengers, we call security. But when a storm rolls in, that's when things get dicey — no one has a direct phone line to Mother Nature.

There's nothing more frustrating for the passengers — or the flight crew — than a weather delay. I remember one in particular that was hairier than most. I noticed when I arrived at the airport for a flight from New Orleans to Atlanta that the flight was thirty minutes delayed. *No big deal,* I thought. So the captain and I boarded the plane and began our preflight checks, making some minor adjustments to account for the time delay.

Then, during the passenger boarding process, and about fifteen minutes prior to our new departure time, I called air traffic control to get our flight plan clearance for New Orleans to Atlanta. I was met with a surprise. "Hey, we've been trying to get ahold of you. All traffic into and out of Atlanta has been stopped due to weather delays. The next Atlanta update will be in an hour." *Great,* I thought, as I grabbed hold of the radio controls to give an already inconvenienced cabin some unwelcome news. I announced that we were going to let them deplane so they could get comfortable while we awaited further information. (And yes, I heard every grumble as people walked past the front cabin door.)

Well, the hour passed relatively quickly, and then, right after we boarded again — wouldn't you know it — the news came that the delay was still in effect. I was beginning to get the sense that we all were in for a very, very long night. I was about to grab the radio control to commiserate with the passengers in the cabin, but then I had a better idea. Rather than motivate the cabin through misery ("I know, this stinks, I want to get home too. Come on, let's hang together and we'll get through this"), I decided to try a new approach. What did the cabin need right now? Information? What didn't I have? Information. But what *did* I have? Reassurance that we were doing everything we could. Knowing the message would have a greater impact delivered in person, I left the cockpit and started walking down the aisles.

I began by grabbing everyone's attention with a full apology. Then I explained the situation in detail and said that I was committed to getting passengers to their destination. I mentioned the flight attendants would make additional passes through the cabin with snacks and beverages to ensure that everyone's needs were met. Finally, I shared that as soon as we could leave, I'd alert everyone so we could clean up the cabin and get going.

I then decided to take questions and address people's concerns, which mostly involved details of air traffic control and weather. Some people wanted Delta pilot wings to give to their grandchildren, and fortunately we had those on board. I even gave my cell phone to someone whose battery had died so he could check his connections. And before too long—wouldn't you know it—I was collecting more of people's travel horror stories.

I've got to admit that I didn't do much more than be as informative as possible and empathize with some frustrated people, but I was surprised by how, after that walk, the angry buzz in the cabin died down. When we finally announced takeoff, people cheered, and then they cheered even louder when we landed—seven hours late—in Atlanta.

What really surprised me was how many sincere thank-yous I received from passengers leaving the airplane. In fact, when I was walking through the airport later, a couple approached me and shared their appreciation for the crew and me for doing the best we could and getting them home, even if it was a half-day later than expected. You can bet that I, in turn, thanked them for flying the friendly skies.

SPARK ACTIONS

To demonstrate service-based leadership:

- Consistently be focused on understanding the needs of others and working hard to meet them. Service-based leadership isn't a onetime event.
- Seek to serve *first*. Don't make people have to ask you for support and assistance.

- Sometimes the simplest actions are all it takes to be of service to others.
- Don't just *think* about serving others — do it. We often have good intentions that fall to the wayside because we can't find time to serve others. Even five minutes a day is enough to have a positive impact on others.

CHARGING AHEAD

Service-oriented cultures don't emerge on their own. It takes Sparks to create conditions where everyone helps each other and works together to achieve organizational objectives.

Service starts with you — and the little things you can do day in and day out to help build teamwork. We're here to help with the following resources on www.sparkslead.us:

- *Culture:* What type of organization do you work in? This quiz is designed to get you and your colleagues thinking about the type of culture you experience currently and the type of culture you'd like to experience. This will allow you and your team to discuss what you each can do to build the environment that will be most beneficial and rewarding to all.
- *Leadership Laboratory:* An ounce of service goes a long way! This exercise is designed to get you building the service habit. If you can dedicate a week to serving others intentionally, you'll be able to see quickly the impact you can have on others.

Small acts of service can transform relationships, teams, and cultures. And when you're the Spark who pulls people together to form a team, everyone wins. As you begin to develop your service efforts, you might discover that there's another quality that will help you take greater actions on behalf of others — confidence. Whenever you're developing new behaviors, an ounce of confidence can go a long way, which is why the next chapter comes right on time.

7

BUILD YOUR CONFIDENCE

Your confidence level will determine the level of results you experience. Sparks don't leave their confidence to chance. They consciously manage their internal thought process to achieve a level of steadiness as their sense of confidence rises.

Y OUR EXPERIENCES, EDUCATION, talents, and skills will take you far in life. They'll help you build an impressive résumé and open doors to opportunities. But what's the one quality that will get you even further and help you capitalize on whatever life presents you? Confidence.

Confidence is absolutely essential.

Confidence is your belief in your abilities. It's the feeling that you can rise to the occasion when the pressure is on. It not only fuels your ambition but encourages you to set stretch goals. It even has a powerful influence on the results you experience. As the great Henry Ford once said, "If you think you can, or think you can't, you're right."

We all want confidence, especially during those critically important moments when we feel like so much is on the line and our actions will make or break our future — for instance, during an interview for our ideal job, or a meeting with a client to close a deal. But to have confidence in these clutch moments, we need to first understand its nature.

Confidence isn't a skill, like biking, typing, or juggling balls. A skill is something you only have to learn once and then you've pretty much got it for the rest of your life. Confidence is an emotion, which helps explain why it wavers at times (or is sometimes entirely absent when you need it the most). It's shaky confidence that makes you sometimes feel like you're on a roller coaster — experiencing highs upon receiving great news and then plummeting a few seconds later back into the valley of insecurity.

As we've explained so far in *Spark*, there is so little we control in life. But we can control our confidence. Confidence, like any Spark behavior, can be developed and managed. It starts with employing the right strategies on your Spark journey, which include:

- Experiencing success
- Developing positive self-appraisals
- Surrounding yourself with positive role models
- Managing confidence-killing emotions

When you build and develop your confidence, over time you start to see yourself differently — as strong and capable, not fearful and uncertain. Before you know it, you find yourself engaging in new pursuits because you have a renewed appreciation for your abilities. You start to explore your untapped potential as your confidence grows. What's more, when one confident Spark emerges, others take notice. Everyone wants to be on the team when a confident leader is at the helm. Sparks who exude confidence tend to assert their opinions persuasively, they challenge the status quo because they're not afraid to make things better, and they thrive in ambiguity because they believe they can lead themselves — and others — through it.

To examine where you are on the confidence continuum, the best place to start is by thinking about your successes in life and how you handled them. Did you *achieve* your successes . . . or did you *experience* them? The difference might sound nuanced, but it's very profound.

BUILDING CONFIDENCE ONE EXPERIENCE AT A TIME

Sean's Story

We've all achieved successes throughout our lives. Some have been significant, like earning a college degree, winning an award, or being selected for a promotion. Some have been less momentous, like planning a great party, kicking a goal in a soccer game, or mowing the perfect lawn. But regardless of the magnitude of your successes, it's important to experience them.

Experiencing success is an internal response to your achievements. It's taking the time to recognize that *your* results are due to *your* efforts. It's not bravado — walking around proud as a peacock because of something great you've done and putting your ego on parade by telling everyone how awesome you are. Rather, it's a quiet, personal, reflective moment when you simply get to congratulate yourself on your accomplishments. It's saying to yourself, *Hey, you worked hard. You earned this,* when you did something meaningful.

When you take the time to acknowledge and experience your achievements, you have ready points of reference for success to summon and help you feel stronger when you're feeling challenged — when you need your confidence to get you through a difficult spot. When you're going into a tough negotiation, or you're getting ready to have a difficult conversation with a colleague, you can recall quickly: *I've felt like this before. And when I did, I came out on top. I can do this again.*

Referencing your successes in critical times is a surefire way to reclaim your confidence. I know this from experience. One memorable time I had to do this was when I was transitioning out of the Air Force and into Delta Airlines.

Some might think that after flying an F-16 fighter, I'd find it easy to fly any other aircraft. I kind of thought that too. After flying a high-performing, fast-moving airplane, I thought flying a slow, bulky 737 was going to be as easy as driving a minivan. And with a copilot by my side to "share" my job, I mistakenly believed that my role at Delta would require half the effort the Air Force required.

The truth is, I was in for a huge slice of humble pie when I started at Delta and found myself struggling in the 737 flight simulator. I could take off just fine and keep the plane in flight, but my landings were something no passenger would ever want to experience. I was also learning new procedures in the cockpit that were very different from the ones I had learned in the Air Force. I felt like I couldn't "unlearn" my old way of doing things fast enough. I also was surprised at how exhausted I was after my training sessions, owing to the level of conscious effort I was pouring into developing these new skills. When I left training and returned home, I felt frustrated and discouraged because things weren't going as smoothly as I had hoped. To say my confidence was shaken would be an understatement, but I was fortunate to have an advantage during this time. I had a string of successes I could reflect on to pull myself through this tough spot.

When I'd get home and go for a walk to catch some fresh air, rather than dwell on what I couldn't do, sink into a slump, or question whether I should have even made the career transition, I'd spend time reflecting on what I'd done before to overcome pressure. I recalled all the previous times I'd felt uncertain and nervous — like flying complex sorties in the Air Force or even competing in high school sports — and thought about what I did to get myself through those times. Mostly, I'd remember, I had focused on the fundamentals and accepted feedback to help strengthen my performance.

I then thought about how I could do the same with what I was experiencing right then. Just going through this process refreshed my perspective on my current situation, helped me find an inner resolve, and prepared me for the next day of training . . . and then the next day after that, and so on and so forth. Ultimately, by regularly repeating this exercise, I completed training and felt confident in the cockpit and ready to lead crews and passengers in the 737.

My confidence development certainly didn't stop there. Confidence is a necessary lifelong pursuit and even more important for us to have as we become more mature in our careers. As we grow and develop we find ourselves constantly taking on more responsibilities, and the stakes become higher. Our failures, missteps, and missed expectations don't just involve us — we have families to support, teams who depend on us, and employers who are expecting us to solve their problems when the answers to their challenges aren't clear. We need to have a reliable, dependable source of personal confidence to help ourselves and others through uncertainty and unexpected crises. Furthermore, this source of confidence has to be real.

YOU REALLY CAN'T FAKE IT UNTIL YOU MAKE IT

There's a popular phrase these days that you've probably heard before — "Fake it till you make it." That might work in certain situations, but when it comes to confidence development, this strategy is flawed in its design. Pretending to be someone you're not isn't going to help you be the person you need to be when the pressure is on.

As a Spark, empty or baseless beliefs in your abilities can't help you generate self-trust and self-reliance. Confidence is about seeing yourself clearly, appreciating your abilities, and having a solid foundation on which to build when presented with challenges. There's nothing more solid than concrete examples of past successes.

You also need these examples when you bump up against an important truth in life: sometimes you won't come out on top. While our confidence will get us in the arena and help us hold our own in a fight, that's not to say we'll always win. The reality is that we might not get the promotion, we could get laid off, or we might lose the sale. But this is where we need our confidence — *real confidence* — more than ever. Real confidence allows us to endure setbacks and persevere as we're trying to make sense of what the heck just happened and figure out what we're going to do next.

To start experiencing success, be conscious of your successful moments and bookmark them — don't run past them. Also, always be sure to attribute your success to *yourself*, not to someone else or some random event or luck. Branch Rickey, the notable baseball executive who brought Jackie Robinson to the big leagues, once observed, "Luck is the residue of design." Meaning that, if you work hard and prepare hard enough, there's a good chance that good fortune will smile on you.

Hard work and preparation not only help you catalog your success but also fend off the Imposter Syndrome — a psychological phenomenon even the most successful, talented, and accomplished professionals experience at peaks in their careers. It's a feeling that your success isn't really due to your own hard work but rather merely a result of other people, or other circumstances, and you just happened to be nearby to catch some of the glow of others' shining moments.

We've worked with a client who diligently counters the Imposter Syndrome with her "Gold Star" system, which she developed after attending one of our Leadership Boot Camps. While learning about confidence, she realized that she never experienced her professional success. What was worse, she was guilty of thinking that success found her, not the other way around. Upon reflecting on how she could build confidence, she realized that the last time in her life she really felt successful was in grade school. "I used to go home and put my gold-starred papers on the refrigerator," she said. "That was such a point of pride for me! But these days, I don't have a professional equivalent." So she made one up. Now, whenever she feels she's done something well or hit a milestone, she gives herself a mental Gold Star. Though it's not a tangible item, it feels real to her, and it's an effective way for her to keep track of all the great things she's done.

As you can see, so much of confidence is being conscious of how you handle your success *and* managing your internal dialogue when those moments occur. This leads us to our next confidence-building action: developing positive self-appraisals.

CRICKETS

Angie's Story

When Courtney and I were doing research on confidence, what piqued my interest was the concept of *self-talk* — the idea that the words we mutter in our minds have a strong influence over our performance. "Geez, that sounds so cheesy when you say it. I mean, who talks to themselves?" Courtney commented. And then, as we started thinking about times when we'd talked to ourselves, we broke into laughter. "You got me! Apparently I talk to myself all the time," she confided.

The fact is, we all talk to ourselves all the time. But what words do we use — are they self-promoting or self-defeating? To build confidence, Sparks develop the discipline to have positive self-appraisals.

If there's any of the four confidence-building qualities I struggle with the most, it's this one. I'm sometimes shocked how often I'm not on my own side. When I become conscious of these self-doubting talk tracks, I correct them — but I'm always surprised that my default appraisals aren't always very positive.

And these self-appraisals definitely affect my confidence, limiting how boldly I take action.

Let me explain. When Courtney and I first started our business, we knew that training and development was going to require *a lot* of public speaking. While we felt up to the task, that didn't mean we weren't nervous. I can remember many early "gigs" when we would huddle together prior to our engagement and give each other mini pep talks to get ready for the presentation.

One memorable experience was when we were speaking at the *Atlanta Business Journal* Conference in front of more than 2,000 professionals and were following a presentation by the leadership guru John Maxwell. This was now the largest audience we'd ever been in front of. Having read Maxwell's books and worshiped his work, it was unnerving to be on the same bill as him. I remember sharing with Courtney, "I hope we don't suck." She smacked me on the arm. "That's the wrong attitude," she reminded me. "Let's just go out there and do our best — we can do this."

Were we awesome that day? Well, that's up to the audience to decide. How did I feel? In fact, pretty confident. I've found that the right attitude, coupled with the right internal dialogue, can make things happen in life. The wrong attitude, however, combined with self-doubting dialogue, can stop you in your tracks and make you want to run home and hide your head.

I can recall one professional experience when this was really clear to me. It was during a board meeting for a Marine Corps nonprofit where I served as one of the directors. During the meeting, the chairman was challenging all members to think differently about fund-raising. He pushed us, "What are we not doing to help fund our organization's mission? Can anyone think of anything that we haven't considered?"

Well, I had an idea. I've spent a lot of time inside organizations helping them develop diversity strategies to drive organizational results. Scanning the boardroom, it was clear to me that our board composition could be more diverse. I was the only woman and the youngest member, all the members were Caucasian, and all, except one, had served in the Marine Corps. It was clear that we were just too much alike. How could we think differently, innovatively, and creatively when in so many ways we all had similar points of view?

I raised my hand and said to the chairman, "I think one of our challenges is the lack of diversity represented on our board. There's more than enough data to support that diverse boards deliver stronger results — financial and otherwise. This is true in the corporate world, and I can't imagine why it would be different in the nonprofit world." After sharing some facts and figures to support my perspective, I finished up and then sat up in my seat a little bit straighter, proud that I'd made my case so strongly. Then I waited for a reply. And waited . . . and waited. Scanning the reactions of my fellow board members, I just couldn't get a read on them. That was when my confident pride faded to insecurity. *Oh dear God,* I thought. *What have I done?*

The chairman, an amazing leader and consummate gentleman, then broke the silence: "Angie, thank you for that.

That's something I've never considered. Does anyone have any thoughts?" And then there it was — more silence. You could hear crickets. Rarely did this board *not* have an opinion. Yet there we were, and I felt insecure over having raised the issue that silenced the room. I then felt embarrassed, like I had either offended someone or made someone really angry by my bold assertion. Or that maybe I had tarnished the reputation I had been carefully building. When the meeting adjourned, I didn't engage in polite chitchat with the other members but headed straight to the door, caught a cab, and hightailed it to the airport so I could go home and be alone with my self-destructive insecure thoughts.

When I finally got to my gate, I made a beeline for a seat that was farthest away from the main traffic aisle in an attempt to avoid seeing any fellow board members. But wouldn't you know it? As I made my way there, I passed our board's general counsel, a very famous attorney — John Dowd, who authored the *Dowd Report* that led to the suspension of Pete Rose from baseball for life.

"Hi, Angie, why don't you take a seat right here?" he offered as he motioned to the seat right next to him. In truth, it sounded more like a directive than an invitation. Honestly, I didn't want to sit there because I feared he was going to confront me on how out of line I was at the meeting. I just didn't have the energy to defend my point of view in front of such a skilled and accomplished attorney.

But out of respect, I sat down. And immediately he jumped into the conversation with, "I'm glad you brought that point up about diversity. You're right." He then went on to explain that my point had allowed him to reflect on how diversity had affected him in his life. He even shared that he was going to talk with the CEO about the diversity of our board, because we might be missing out on some of its key benefits.

In those moments, John's perspective shed some critical light on my self-talk. He made me realize how hard I had been on myself and how quickly I'd taken the others' silence to mean that they were judging me when maybe they were just thinking and reflecting about something they'd never thought about before. I was amazed by how automatically I'd conjured the worst-case scenario without even considering a best-case scenario. This realization really reinforced for me that I needed to have more confidence in myself and write a new inner dialogue for when I'm feeling stressed or pressured, because the current one wasn't helping. Had I not had this random encounter with John, I would have drowned myself in my own miserable self-talk for weeks.

John and I spent the next thirty to forty minutes talking about our life experiences, diversity, families, and the Marine Corps. It was the beginning of what I consider to be an important mentoring relationship for me. When we were done, he said, "You need to talk with my friend Joe. He needs to hear what you have to say about diversity."

"Joe who?" I asked.

"Dunford," he said.

At the time, General Joseph "Fighting Joe" Dunford didn't need a further introduction — I knew him as the Assistant Commandant of the Marine Corps, the second-highest-ranking Marine in the organization. And considering the Marine Corps was just beginning to study the integration of women into ground combat roles, a meeting with him regarding diversity couldn't have been more timely.

True to his word, John made the introduction, which led to an invitation to sit down with General Dunford and share my perspectives on diversity with him. He asked for my help in arranging a private luncheon with other Marines and the Commandant of the Marine Corps, who's the CEO-equivalent in the organization, and his executive team. It was a lively, candid, and memorable discussion. My relationship with General Dunford continued as he became Chairman of the Joint Chiefs of Staff, with whom I've now shared my thoughts, ideas, and research on diversity to help promote a military in which everyone — from recruit to active-duty service member to Veteran — recognizes the benefits that diversity can bring to an organization.

When I look back on the string of events that allowed me to provide my perspectives on diversity to the highest levels of the military, there's no doubt that confidence has been a part of every step. This Spark quality inspired me to speak my mind and share my point of view, even though I had mistakenly told myself that it had been received poorly. In fact, speaking up opened the door to greater opportunities.

What has sustained me as a Spark is the ability to manage my confidence by substituting positive self-appraisals for those harmful, negative ones. I'm not perfect at this — I'm still a work in progress — but I lean on this story about John Dowd and General Dunford for confidence boosting all the time.

THE WORDS WE TELL OURSELVES

Developing positive self-appraisals begins with paying attention to our thoughts, which can be difficult to do because it's hard to stop a train of thought that's already barreling down its tracks. This is where cognitive discipline comes in. As we listen to our inner dialogue, it's important to separate the words, phrases, and mantras that are helpful from those that are damaging and could derail us from becoming a Spark.

When we catch these self-defeating appraisals, we have to hold them in our minds and reframe them. For example, imagine that you need to confront your boss on an important issue that you disagree with him about. Rather than say to yourself, *It's hopeless — I can't do it. It's not really my place to disagree with his remarks on my performance review,* stop yourself and rewrite your script: *If I don't stand up for myself, no one else will. He should know that I don't agree with how my performance is being characterized.*

When you find that you're beating yourself up, stop in the moment and start down a new path, one where you begin to promote yourself and all the great things you've done. When you refresh your memory about your accomplishments, you start to feel like a Spark who is prepared to face whatever comes your way.

There are always going to be times when you find you're being particularly hard on yourself. That is when you just need to have a Stuart Smalley moment. Remember that beloved *Saturday Night Live* character? Rather than tear yourself down, build yourself up by reaffirming, *You're good enough, smart enough, and doggone it, people like you.* (You're allowed to substitute your own words for the Smalley appraisal, but you get the point.)

The research that supports positive self-appraisals is quite compelling. Albert Bandura, the well-known psychologist at Stanford University, spent a great portion of his career studying the concept of self-efficacy, which is the belief in your capabilities and the impact of that belief on your environment and outcomes. His research sparked myriad other research projects (primarily on athletes), and most have reached the conclusion that you can have a tremendous impact on outcomes just by what you choose to tell yourself in the moments when confidence is needed. While it might sound like a subtle difference, there's a major distinction between "I hope I get hired" and

"I should get hired because my career results speak for themselves." What you believe will have a direct impact on what you achieve. With the right dialogue, the results will follow.

While it's important to be able to rely on yourself in those moments that count, this next strategy helps you also rely on others who can help you develop and promote your confidence.

SURROUND YOURSELF WITH POSITIVE ROLE MODELS

Courtney's Story

So much of your Spark journey will require you to put yourself "out there," such as by leading a committee, improving a skill that you've long considered a weakness, or confronting a colleague on a sensitive issue. Growth is great, but it's natural to experience vulnerability as you develop new habits and take on more challenges. During this time, you might even grapple with uncertainty as you wait to see how your risks pan out. These are the vital moments when your confidence is truly on the line. It's also susceptible to other people's opinions, some of which aren't going to be positive.

In a perfect world, no one would judge or question you, but our worlds are far from perfect. Be cautious in these moments about who you let influence your powerful, important opinion of yourself. If it's anyone and everyone, your confidence will wane, if not crumble altogether.

At the same time, however, our confidence needs to be influenced by someone — or a team of someones. Our confidence can be bolstered by individuals who care about us and have our best interests at heart. We need positive role models in our lives because we're stronger and better with their counsel.

Positive role models are rare, but they do exist. They may not be the loudest voices in the room, but they're the ones we need to listen to — especially when what they're telling us that we need to hear is very different from what we want to hear. They're the ones who'll say to you, "I know you want to tell your boss off, but don't," or, "You really need to apply for that job. It might feel like a leap, but it's important to do it right now."

I've benefited from having many of these "truth-brokers" in my life who haven't held their opinions back and have helped by challenging me, being constructive, or presenting an alternative point of view. Sure, they can be cheerleaders too, but I don't seek them out for that reason. I value honesty and candor in my relationships, and I've grown the most by listening to the people who have pushed my thinking and guided me toward a better result.

One of these individuals is a high school friend's dad, Bob Turner. After selling his business to a *Fortune* 500 company, Bob transitioned to an executive role at an international information technology firm. He's given me great advice at every twist and turn in my career, such as during the early days of Lead Star.

Starting a business is exciting. When Angie and I were getting Lead Star off the ground, we were having a great time naming our firm, selecting a logo, developing the website, and talking about our vision. We had so many ideas and expectations for success, but we had very few conversations about our long-term strategy and the mechanics of running the business. It's not that these conversations weren't important; they just weren't as much fun as the others. But it wasn't even a concern of mine until a chance encounter with Bob at a local party.

As soon as I saw Bob I couldn't wait to tell him about Lead Star. I knew he'd share in my enthusiasm and offer some great advice. So I approached him and started gushing about my firm and my ideas. Bob, who served in the Marines, kept nodding during our conversation, which I interpreted initially as: *This is great, I love the concept! Tell me more.*

But then, after listening to me for a few minutes, he stopped me in midsentence and said, "Courtney, I've advised a lot of young entrepreneurs at this stage in their businesses. The best advice I can offer you at this point is 'cash is king.' Your idea is solid, but just watch your cash flow." He then got into the nuts and bolts of financing and forecasting and kept asking me in-depth questions about strategy that I didn't have answers to. The tone of our conversation took a very sobering turn. I left the party not too long after, feeling a sense of angst as I absorbed all of Bob's questions. It's not that I didn't appreciate what he offered; it's just that his guidance wasn't exactly what I'd expected or hoped for.

Bob's feedback took me aback, but in many ways it also propelled me forward. When Lead Star's honeymoon phase ended shortly after our conversation, his guidance came in handy, because no matter how awesome our website or our company logo was, our services weren't going to sell themselves. Angie and I needed to get down to business and start generating revenue. I remember thinking to myself during this time, *Cash is king*, and smiling as I thought about how perfect the guidance was and how unready I was to receive it when I did.

Looking back, I see now that Bob's guidance helped me cut through my raw enthusiasm so I could focus on getting the business off the ground. My confidence grew as I started to realize the benefits of his counsel and anticipate the guidance he would offer next. I've discovered that his advice was also great at preventing me from getting overconfident; that feeling often arises when we have no one in our life who keeps us in check. Bob always seems to be two steps ahead of me and has an uncanny way of presenting wisdom at times when I need it the most.

RECOGNIZING POSITIVE ROLE MODELS

The problem, of course, is that valuable role models don't walk into our lives saying, "Hi, I'm here to help!" As Sparks, we need to go find them. That quest starts with being able to recognize them when we see them.

The best way you can pinpoint positive role models is to reflect on the Spark behaviors we've presented so far and think about the people you know who embody them. These are people who are credible, accountable, and service-oriented, who have solid character and seem trustworthy. It's only natural on your Spark journey to seek to be surrounded and supported by people like this.

Once you identify the people in your own life who exhibit Spark behavior, you have to develop these relationships, regardless of where you are in your career. And by the way, more mature professionals need role models just as much as early career professionals do. Just because we may now be serving as mentors doesn't mean our need for positive role models vanishes. It still exists, and it can be fulfilled in many ways, such as through an outside organization like a professional club, alumni association, or board of directors.

These relationships also need to be nurtured. As a Spark, engage the people you admire and respect on a consistent basis, whether through conversations over coffee or ongoing email exchanges. One colleague of ours makes it a point to schedule two lunches each month with different people she admires. Her conversations with them don't have an agenda; this is simply her way of maintaining the relationships she's worked so hard to build.

Finally, we have to be open to input. If our role models are challenging us, that's a great thing. We need to get uncomfortable in order to develop. Sparks are all about change, but no matter how much we want it, change isn't easy. It can be made easier by a focused effort to develop our confidence.

MANAGING CONFIDENCE-KILLING EMOTIONS

Courtney's Story

Up until this point, we've presented three conscious and deliberate actions you can take to help build your confidence: experiencing your success, developing positive self-appraisals, and surrounding yourself with positive role models. These are actions you can take when you're pushing yourself, experimenting with new behaviors, and trying new things. But these aren't the only times when you need confidence.

Sometimes you'll feel forced to do something you've never done before and you just won't know what to do. Maybe you'll be "pushed" into a management role. Maybe you'll get fired or be demoted in a corporate reorganization. The challenge might be getting selected to lead your organization through a critical initiative, or receiving negative feedback from a client or customer. Perhaps an economic downturn will disrupt your business, or you'll be met with a personal challenge, like going through a divorce.

These are all significant, life-changing experiences that can rattle the inner confidence of even the most accomplished leader. During difficult times like these, the confidence-killing emotions — fear, worry, and insecurity — can sink in and make you question yourself and doubt your true abilities.

I've been coaching executives for many years. One important conclusion I've drawn is that no one is immune to fear, worry, and insecurity. These strong emotions often emerge when we feel we don't have a choice in our circumstances and we're incredibly uncertain about how we're ever going to come out on top again.

Each of these confidence-killing emotions has an antidote that I've tried and tested during the most tumultuous times in my own life. I'm proof that these antidotes work, but that's not to say they're easy to implement. They have to be administered when you're experiencing these emotions at their peak and your mental agility isn't the strongest. For me, this was right after my husband Patrick and I welcomed our identical twin daughters into the world and also received news that shook our foundation.

We were as prepared as we could have been for our girls' arrival. Patrick had taken a leave of absence from his career at the fire department to focus on the girls full-time and be the dad-on-duty when I traveled for work. We also had an impressive plan to manage our two beautiful bundles of joy — color-coded clothes to help our friends tell the girls apart; a logbook to keep track of every feeding, diaper change, and fever; and an intense sleep training schedule to get the girls' nighttime rhythms in sync. We even had contingency plans in the event that our initial plans didn't work out. Believe me, we had quite the operation going. But about a month into parenthood we learned that we couldn't plan for everything.

As our family was settling into our routine I received some devastating news from my mother, who lived nearby: she had been diagnosed with leukemia and her prognosis was uncertain. Just like that, my life turned on a dime. I didn't know it at the time, but my first six months of being a mom would be the last six months I'd have with my mother.

All the joy and excitement I was experiencing as a new mom

was sapped and replaced by fear, worry and insecurity. I didn't know what to do, and I had no rulebook to reference. In the weeks that followed my mom's diagnosis, these raw emotions took over. I was afraid of what my mom was going through and what fighting cancer would mean for her. *How painful will it be? What will she need to feel better?* I also feared for my new-born daughters, whose new mother was frazzled and having to split her time between them and her own mom. I also feared for my work. Lead Star was still a small, growing business, and without the full attention of its two owners, it was certain to falter. I couldn't risk that.

I became consumed with worry. Each minute of the day I worried about my mom, my daughters, or my business, and when I wasn't worrying I became worried about not worrying. Everything in life felt so frail. It seemed like if I wasn't thinking about it, I wasn't caring for it.

I also felt insecure, which was a surprising emotion for me. Normally I'm a fairly confident person, but insecurity had a powerful leveling effect on me. In those insecure moments, I felt like everything I was doing was wrong. It almost seemed like I had a voice whispering in my ear all day long, questioning whether I was doing all I could for my daughters, for my mom, for my business partner, for our clients. I felt pulled in every direction and torn among all my responsibilities. I felt insecure about even thinking about work when my mother's life was at risk. I was insecure about supporting a family, and the responsibility seemed overwhelming.

I wanted to be everything for everyone, but I just couldn't pull it off. I couldn't muster the energy and I couldn't create enough time in my day. Before too long, I was in the throes of a full-blown confidence crisis. I just didn't believe I had what it took to overcome all the challenges I was managing. Or trying to manage. All of the past successes I had experienced seemed meaningless at that point. I wasn't sure if I was capable of making it through the day in front of me, let alone being of value to anyone else.

But as my mom grew sicker, my reality became clearer. I knew I had to dig deeper to find the strength to keep going. I didn't have a choice over what I was experiencing, but I did have a choice over how I responded to what was happening in my life. I had to be brutally honest with myself. I started by thinking about what I was feeling and what I was afraid of. Just beginning to name my fears helped my courage start taking over.

I needed to stop reacting and start responding. I knew that I couldn't do everything on my own and I needed help. That simple admission was enough to get me thinking that I needed to formulate a real plan—just as I'd responded when I was shocked to learn I was pregnant with twins.

My husband and I started talking in detail about what we needed to do to ensure that our children and family were secure and that my mom had everything she needed to be as comfortable as possible. We started to take "shifts" with our daughters and my mom. I even reached out to nearby friends and family members, asking them to make treks to the hospital to see my mom or stop by the house to hold a baby. I was amazed at how people stepped in and helped out. At work, I also relied heavily on my Lead Star team—they were most understanding and pitched in where they could.

In the end, however, I was the only who could experience the amazement and challenges of motherhood, witness my mother's passing, and run my business. To muster confidence to take on all of these roles, I had to demonstrate a tremendous amount of emotional discipline—to not hide from this experience and the full range of emotions that came with it, but to embrace it and make the most of it. Each day I took time to experience any small success — the girls sleeping more than six hours at a time, being able to watch a movie at the hospital with my mom (and staying awake until the end), responding to email at work in a timely manner to keep my livelihood intact. I also focused on my inner dialogue, reminding myself that what I was dealing with was hard, but not impossible. I also had some great people in my life who cheered me on and supported me as I worked through all the uncertainty.

About a month prior to my mom's death, we received news that at the time seemed so joyful: her cancer was in remission. Unfortunately, the good news would not last. Her heart could not handle the final consolidation round of chemotherapy given to patients to destroy any remaining cancer cells. Just weeks after being told she was in remission, she suffered congestive heart failure and was placed on life support in the cardiac ICU.

As the end drew near for my mom, my confidence, already being severely tested, continued to be tested even more. My mother had designated me as her proxy for all medical decisions at the point when she would no longer be able to make them herself. During the last days of her life, I had to work closely with my sister as we worked through my mother's care and agreed on a plan.

I grew as a person by being able to be full and present with all the responsibilities in front of me. Looking back, I know I did the best I could in circumstances that were more than daunting.

I know I'm not the first (or last) person to suffer the loss of a parent. And I know I'm not the only one who's experienced challenge and pain. I offer my story as a way to share and acknowledge that we all experience difficult times in our lives. When these times are upon us, we need to face the fear, worry, and insecurity that will accompany them. By understanding how these natural emotions affect our ability to move forward confidently in the face of crisis, we are better prepared to respond to them. And while we won't come through hardship unscathed, we can come out more resilient and better prepared for the next inevitable challenge on the horizon.

COMBATING CONFIDENCE-KILLING EMOTIONS

One of our colleagues talks openly about fear, which can seem a bit taboo considering his background. Alex has served on the most elite Navy SEAL teams, has led countless combat operations, and has trained future SEAL officers at the Naval Academy. We like to think of our warriors as fearless, but Alex is quick to remind anyone that fears are natural and that they're driven by our instincts. We need to pay attention to them — not succumb to them — because they're telling us we need to take action in order to stay alive. So when Alex feels a pit in his stomach, he doesn't ignore it. To him, it's an important alert, like a pink flag that's about to turn red. He knows that this is the time when he needs to demonstrate courage, which isn't action in the absence of fear — it's action in the face of it.

Courage can be either physical or moral, but however it's manifested, it needs to be evoked and executed, because it's the only way to positively influence your circumstances.

We all have our own internal signals that we're experiencing fear. Though our survival might not be threatened, our security, stability, and long-term success could very well be. When we have these fear responses, we need to tune in to them. Just by paying attention to our emotions, we can identify when we're feeling anxious, and when we do, we can't ignore that emotion.

We have to confront it. Sometimes asking ourselves a simple question (*What can I do about this right now?*) is enough to propel us toward action.

To combat worry, another confidence-killing emotion that is often induced by stress, it's important to determine whether your concerns are real or manufactured. Our brains, even as brilliant as they can be, often have a hard time distinguishing between the two. Sometimes, when left unattended, your imagination can run wild, and what you're worrying about is neither logical nor rational. You can quickly find yourself worrying about things that can't possibly happen, or that are even well beyond your ability to influence.

When you find yourself in a worried state, ask yourself, *Is this real? If so, can I solve it?* The answers to these questions should help you figure out what actions — if any — you can take to manage your worries. And if you can't affect the situation you're in, tell yourself, *I'm not worried. I'm just concerned.* Being concerned about something is an acknowledgment that you're aware of the predicament but there's little you can do to influence it. So rather than worry about whether it will rain on your friend's wedding day, or whether your child will get accepted into the college of her choice, remind yourself that you're merely concerned and that there's nothing you can do to change the outcome. Maintaining your perspective is key.

To deal with the confidence-killing emotion of insecurity, it's helpful to refer back to the second confidence-building strategy: developing positive self-appraisals. Whenever you experience insecurity, you need to tame and quiet your inner critic. You need to flip your criticisms of yourself and offer yourself praise instead. Rather than beat yourself down, pause in the moment and recall all the things you've done, all the milestones you've achieved, and say to yourself, *I can do this.* This mental reminder can often be enough to get you back on the confidence-building track that gets your head back in the game.

SPARK ACTIONS

Confidence is an emotion that Sparks can manage. To achieve a steady level of confidence:

- Recognize that insecurity can often accompany success. It's critical to acknowledge how your talents directly connect to the successes you experience.
- Pay attention to what you tell yourself during moments when you feel pressure. Often, rewriting any negative internal dialogue can give you the confidence you need to get through a challenge.
- Surround yourself with truth-brokers. We need people in our lives who tell us what we *need* to hear, not what we *want* to hear.

CHARGING AHEAD

As a Spark, you need to build and manage your confidence intentionally. Here are several resources on www.sparkslead.us that will help you reflect on the subject and formulate a plan:

- *Confidence Moments:* What have been the most successful moments in your life? What were the circumstances, and when did you experience these successes? Just going through the process of identifying moments when your actions — not the actions of others — contributed to your success allows you to appreciate what you've done and gives you fuel for all the work that's left undone.

- *Positive Appraisals:* We can undermine our best efforts quickly by not paying attention to what we tell ourselves when we feel challenged, pressured, or stressed. This exercise gives you tactics you can employ to help rewrite negative internal dialogue.

Raising your confidence level will help you get into the mindset that's essential for the final Spark behavior: demonstrating consistency.

8

DEMONSTRATE CONSISTENCY

Sparks set a high standard for consistency in their everyday work. To achieve it, they first need to understand the value of readiness, know what perseverance really means, and have the courage to "own" their time.

B EING A SPARK REQUIRES that you be clear about your values, intentions, credibility, and confidence. Only when you know what types of behaviors truly reflect who you are — and what you are capable of — can you be a Spark. To become a Spark you must develop and demonstrate a real sense of consistency in every aspect of your life.

Consistency is your ability to always adhere to your values and intentions regardless of your circumstances. It determines whether you're a "sometimes person" or an "always person." Sometimes people are those whose behavior you just can't anticipate. *Will he show up on time? Will he meet this project milestone?* Always people are those whose behavior you can count on. *I know she'll meet the deadline. I have no doubt that she'll impress me with her presentation.*

Being an always person opens the doors to opportunities — high-stakes projects and high-visibility assignments get tasked to those who have proven their dependability. Consistency also contributes to the level of trust you have in all of your relationships, especially the most important one: your relationship with yourself.

Sparks need to be able to trust themselves. *Sparks do what they say they're going to do when they say they'll do it.* This is especially critical when you're developing your Spark behaviors. For example, if you've determined that you need to spend more time developing mentors, or that you need to mind your say-do gap, you have to take action immediately *and* consistently. Your Spark goals shouldn't sit on the back burner for too long—the longer you delay action, the more you distance yourself from your goals, and the less likely you are to achieve them. Also, most goals aren't reached in one attempt—achieving excellence through consistency takes time. The sooner you take initiative the faster you'll create "wins" and form Spark habits. Plus, success—even the smallest of successes—gives you the motivation and energy to keep working on the Spark behavior you're developing.

The alternative to consistency is inconsistency, or a lack of follow-through. Those who are inconsistent break trust with themselves, their good ideas die on the vine, and their self-reliance crumbles. Losing is as much of a habit as winning is, and the outcomes can be fairly severe. Inconsistency can quickly lead to lost opportunity, to a lack of hope, and to despair—a path no Spark wants to explore. What's worse, not being able to trust yourself raises an important question: Why should others put their trust in you?

Your history of dependability and pattern of strong performance make a great case for why others should rely on you. Your consistency makes you the sought-after colleague and all-around go-to person in nearly every environment in which you work. Sparks who have demonstrated consistency are hand-picked for projects, called on for their counsel, and put in the game in the final seconds to score the winning shot.

To begin on your pathway to developing consistency, think about the disciplines you have in place and consider what additional ones you need to develop. What often stands between you and the better future you envision for yourself is simply a lack of routine or habit, which can easily be addressed by planning and execution.

WORK THE PLAN

Sean's Story

Most of us have been involved in business planning. This happens when you get together with your colleagues, set targets, and communicate them to ensure that everyone is aligned. Planning is important, but not as important as its complement: execution. Too many times, considerable energy is spent on plan creation, but too little time is devoted to actual plan implementation. That often happens because when new goals are established, new behaviors need to be demonstrated, and that can make us feel uncomfortable and uncertain. Before too long, we revert to our old ways of doing things because they're familiar, they're satisfying, and they keep our ego safe and out of harm's way.

I was fortunate to "grow up" in an organization — the US Air Force — where there was equal emphasis on both planning and execution. As a result, I had to become used to discomfort. The organization certainly pushed me, but I also pushed myself. I was reminded constantly that my training and development would be supported by the Air Force through its structured programs, but that ultimately it was my responsibility to ensure I was ready to meet any foreseeable or unforeseeable challenge or threat. To uphold the Air Force's motto — "We do the impossible every day" — I had to be sharp. For me, this meant developing a plan around what the organization expected of me and what I expected of myself. The next step was working the plan.

I discovered quickly that if I experienced any doubt or ambiguity about the skills I needed to be developing, a quick look back at my plan would bring all the clarity I needed to take initiative.

I wasn't alone in this constant training and development journey; my colleagues were equally committed. We all shared the same goal: readiness. Readiness is an interesting concept. It isn't a term used in business, but it's used constantly in military communities. It's the idea that you're *always* prepared, physically and mentally. When individuals are ready, the force is ready, and that's how it delivers high performance in the most stressful of all environments: when lives are on the line.

In a way, constant readiness is very similar to always being consistent.

I observed the payoff from disciplined, consistent effort when I was stationed at Osan Air Base in the Republic of Korea during the early 1990s. If you're a history buff, you'll remember that the Korean War was never really resolved. There was a cease-fire, which ended the war, but tensions between the North Koreans and the United States remained for decades after the conflict, and they still persist. To this day, I can easily recall the air of uncertainty and alertness I felt whenever I was flying parallel to the Korean Demilitarized Zone (DMZ).

In addition to the F-16 squadrons stationed at Osan, there were also U-2 spy planes that would fly the DMZ with their sensors pointed north, collecting intelligence for the military. We worked interdependently with these crews and were always available to support them if they needed us on a moment's notice. That was exactly the situation my colleagues and I found ourselves in one night.

I remember being woken up in the middle of the night by an urgent, loud knock on my barracks door. When I answered, I was instructed that all the pilots, mechanics, and support personnel had to report to the squadron immediately. A U-2 flying the DMZ was missing, and first indications were that it had been shot down. I grabbed my gear and raced to the squadron, my mind consumed by the severity of the situation. *Is the pilot at risk for being captured? How long before we launch retaliatory attacks?* We weren't a nation engaged in war at the time, but in those few moments it felt like we were on the verge of being in one.

When I arrived at the squadron it was buzzing with activity as courses of action were developed and operation planning got under way. It wasn't a chaotic environment, but it was extremely tense as priorities were unfolding. The first task was to launch a search-and-rescue mission to retrieve the pilot. The next was to prepare an airstrike, which involved loading up jets with 2,000-pound live bombs and missiles in anticipation of striking back.

To add to the complexity of the situation, the U-2 was down in close proximity to our northern neighbors — the pilot was potentially in North Korean waters. There were large numbers of support personnel in the area, including Army and Navy helicopters and Navy ships, and we needed to coordinate with them in order to find the pilot. Even worse, it was also a very stormy and cloudy night; visibility was difficult even with night-vision equipment. Nevertheless, all the military assets had to move quickly to get on the same page and to synchronize their actions. The consequences of a botched mission were very clear:

we could end up engaging in friendly fire in the confusion or, worse, cross the DMZ and inadvertently provoke an already hostile, unpredictable adversary.

My role in the operation centered on planning, which was a very dynamic task that took a tremendous amount of focus so I could attend to details. Flight paths, radio frequencies, search areas, altitudes, and air speeds had to be determined and relayed to all parties involved in the search. All of this had to happen quickly, with zero room for error. I had never before felt entrusted with so much responsibility, but I knew I was up for it. Constant training and readiness had prepared my colleagues and me for this moment.

My colleagues and I checked, double-checked, and triple-checked our plan and also had extra communication and verification with all parties to ensure that everyone was on the same page. When operations commenced and my planning work was nearly complete, I tuned in to the radio traffic to listen to the mission being executed.

The communications and actions every team displayed were crisp, decisive, and precise. There was no second-guessing, no hesitation, and no panicking. We had never coordinated with Navy surface vessels before, so I was amazed by how seamlessly we operated together. The downed pilot was located and recovered without confusion and swiftly returned to base. The U-2's black box was also recovered. This was an important discovery because later it was revealed that the plane experienced a mechanical failure — *it wasn't shot down.* Knowing that helped tensions simmer down, and we were able to call off our potential retaliatory attack.

All of this action unfolded over the course of minutes, though it felt like hours. When we retreated to the ready room for our debrief, we all had a collective exhale before we began to marvel at what had just happened. It was the most intense operation any one of us had ever experienced. We were impressed by how our team pulled off such complex maneuvering at a moment's notice with so much on the line. We went around the room, talking about our emotions and concerns before we went through the operation for lessons learned that could be applied going forward. We acknowledged our hits, we addressed our misses, and when we were finished, there was no doubt that we all felt a real sense of pride. Our disciplined efforts had allowed us to prevail in a volatile, uncertain, and unpredictable environment. This experience reaffirmed our commitment to readiness, because we all knew that, without consistency, we never would have been able to pull off this amazing feat.

THE DISCOMFORT ZONE

Now, most professionals don't work in extreme environments — those worlds where lives are on the line or one false move could lead to an international incident. But we all work in environments that can be chaotic, unpredictable, and fast-paced, making us feel that our actions can either make or break us, or our teams. In such an environment, you need to have developed strong, consistent habits that will prevent you from losing your way when the pressure is turned up.

All habits begin with taking a risk as you push yourself into your discomfort zone — a place that feels awkward, foreign, and unfamiliar. You've probably been uncomfortable before: going to a party where you don't know anyone, representing your firm at a trade show for the first time, or even approaching someone and asking for a big favor. Most of the time we quickly remedy our discomfort by stopping what we're doing and vowing to never do it again.

But Sparks recognize that false starts aren't going to get them where they need to go. They appreciate that ambiguity and uncertainty are necessary parts of growth. Their perseverance through discomfort leads them to the result they're seeking, as well as to a place where they come out stronger. Resilience is created through the cycle of action, perseverance, and success.

To develop consistency with your Spark goals, a plan is a great starting point, but it's not enough to generate commitment to your goals. You also need to create the context for the change you want to experience. Start by looking at your schedule and seeing if it accommodates the goals you have for yourself — *Do I have the time to do what I say I'm going to do?* If you want to serve on a local board, can you keep up with the rigorous meeting schedule? If you want to volunteer on an HR committee that's reviewing how performance in your organization is managed, does your work schedule allow you that level of flexibility? When you're unable to honor your intentions with action, your level of consistency begins to fall to the wayside. When this happens, you become frustrated with your inability to follow through, and you disappoint others by your lack of predictability.

The next step is setting up contingencies to fall back on in the event that not everything goes as planned. Often we undermine our best intentions by taking an "all or nothing" approach to our goals. If you decide to wake up early to go for a walk before work and it's raining outside, it's important to have an alternative plan for squeezing in a workout before you abandon the goal altogether. If you need to complete a proposal during your morning block but get a surprise call from a client demanding a work product right away, you need to demonstrate flexibility in accomplishing your must-do tasks. In the military we call this "planning for friction." In your life you might call it having a plan B.

As you develop consistency, it's also important to recognize that, however exciting it is to start something new, once the newness wears off, you — and others — can become disengaged quite quickly. This is when your effort and energy are needed most. It's fun and relatively easy to give "lip service" commitment to something you're going to do. We've sat through many team strategy sessions where executives made grand, enthusiastic commitments regarding the following year's initiatives. But then when we checked back with them on their progress a few months later, they revealed that the initiatives just couldn't get off the ground — not because of a lack of desire, but because of a lack of will.

Paul Tough, the author of *How Children Succeed: Grit, Curiosity, and the Hidden Power of Character,* spent time studying the qualities that help children transition into successful adults. Not surprisingly, they're not so different from the qualities that make adults into even more successful adults. Tough's book features Angela Lee Duckworth's research on the concept of grit, which she describes as having passion and perseverance toward long-term goals. Duckworth has been inside major businesses, at educational institutions, and within competitions — like spelling bees — to study what makes people successful and why. She has come to the conclusion that success isn't related to social intelligence or IQ. It comes from just sticking with your goals.

That sense of perseverance, by the way, is a *behavior,* not a talent. Always bear that in mind.

That's not to say that once you develop perseverance you have it for the rest of your life. Persevering is an ongoing, constant effort, and there always will be seasons in your life where you have to recommit to it before you fall victim to one of consistency's archenemies: complacency.

THE EXTRA MILE

Courtney's Story

Like Angie, I'm quite fond of Marine Corps "-isms." One particular saying that stood out to me in training is, "The more you sweat in peace, the less you bleed in war." Upon hearing it for the first time, that idea made perfect sense. Preparation is important, and training ensures you're ready. But *knowing* something and *doing* something can feel very different.

I remember arriving at TBS, the Corps' infantry training school for all officers, and reviewing our schedule. I noticed large blocks of time in the daily and monthly plans carved out for "Rehearsal" and "STEX Rehearsals." *These must be pretty important,* I thought to myself as I imagined what they were all about. But when I found out what they were and experienced them, I lost sight of their importance because they were pretty brutal. These blocks represented long, laborious, monotonous hours of going over and over troop movements, formations, and operational plans as we prepared fictional assaults or humanitarian missions. STEX rehearsals were even worse: STEX stands for Sand Table Exercise, meaning we would move little plastic figures around tables full of sand. I always thought that any civilian observer of these drills would think we looked like children in the playground sandbox.

During this time in my career, I wanted action. Rehearsals were, candidly, very boring. I would have much preferred engaging in the type of nonstop running and commotion you see in Marine Corps recruiting commercials, where Marines are racing toward the sound of chaos. Yet I learned quickly — and was reminded frequently — that the only way you can run toward the sound of chaos and *survive* is if everyone knows what they're doing and the team is coordinated and well rehearsed. As much as I dreaded them, rehearsals became a habit and one that I carried into the field with me and eventually into business.

After I left active duty and started working as a sales team manager in the private sector, I worked hard to never go into a conference ill prepared, never host a team meeting without an agenda, and never even respond to an email haphazardly. This thoughtful, considered approach led me to many great results. Even better, all my team members and clients knew what to expect of me. This rhythm came in especially handy when we were starting Lead Star. It eventually led me to land our very first client, Wal-Mart.

When Angie and I started our business, we knew we had to throw the disciplines we acquired in our military careers into our new venture, because we were creating something out of nothing. No one was around to tell us what to do — we had to determine that ourselves. Part of my self-imposed routine was to start the day off reading the newspaper to see which businesses might be prospective clients. One particular morning a headline jumped right out at me — Wal-Mart was involved in a gender discrimination lawsuit, the largest class-action suit ever. The corporation was number one on the *Fortune* 500 list but, according to the article, could potentially be crippled by the lawsuit.

As I read more, I started to brainstorm how leadership training for store managers could be very helpful in keeping store problems at the store level, without becoming full-blown company problems. With a company as big as Wal-Mart, you get a full cross-section of every demographic and personality; invariably, there will be some people in the organization who demonstrate poor judgment. But if you have strong leaders at every level, those doing the wrong things are more likely to be noticed and the problems they've created can be addressed more swiftly.

I decided Wal-Mart was a prime candidate for Lead Star's services. I knew this was a stretch goal, considering Lead Star had no history of past performance that would appeal to the company, but I went to work nonetheless. I put my lawyer skills to work reading the briefs in the discrimination case. I put my sales skills to work crafting the pitch, including a line around "sending in the Marines." And then I started to cold-call into Wal-Mart until I found the right person to sell to.

My efforts working the phones ultimately led me to the manager responsible for diversity training. By a stroke of luck, her father happened to have served in the Marines. I had an "in." After several minutes, she shared, "Courtney, I see Lead Star's value here at Wal-Mart. Let's keep this conversation going." When we wrapped up the call, we agreed to explore finding the right opportunity for Lead Star to work with Wal-Mart. After a few more calls, Lead Star was slated to deliver leadership workshops for Wal-Mart to commemorate Women's History Month. I could hardly contain my excitement — we had just landed our first client, and wow, was it a big one!

Leveraging Wal-Mart as a client quickly led to other work. Burger King was client number two. Cardinal Health soon followed. Preparation and consistent action kept fueling our results.

You know, it's funny — you'd think I never would have forgotten that simple formula. But I did.

Flash-forward about seven years from the day we landed Wal-Mart. I took a late-afternoon flight from the East Coast to San Francisco for an initial in-person meeting with Google. They'd already contracted with us to develop workshops for their high-potential managers in one of their best-performing business units. I don't remember feeling cocky going into the meeting, but even I recognized at the time that I was way too comfortable. I was also pretty exhausted from having been many days on the road, so on the airplane I took a nap instead of diligently preparing, as I had done hundreds of times before.

When my team and I arrived the next morning at Google's impressive headquarters, I couldn't quite pinpoint what was wrong, but I felt off. When the meetings started, I had enough presence to know that, while I was physically there, I wasn't really "there." I had difficulty reading the client, I wasn't quick on my feet responding to questions, and my typical high energy was unusually low that day. Overall, my performance fell flat — I'd give myself an F. It was the absolute worst sales and credibility moment of my career. Lead Star didn't lose the work, but a few days later the client made it clear that they didn't want to work with *me*. Ouch. Not only did that sting in the moment, but it haunted me for weeks to come.

Looking back on this experience, it wasn't like I sabotaged myself intentionally by ignoring the importance of being ready. But when I examined the events leading up to the meeting, I can easily see in hindsight how I put myself at a disadvantage. For starters, I abandoned the fundamental behaviors that had allowed me to be successful up until that point. I created conditions for inconsistency, which led to complacency — I thought I could just wing it and all would be well. That's the workplace equivalent of winning a spot on the Olympic team but then failing to show up for practice to prepare for the games.

I also failed to carve out space in my calendar ahead of time to prepare and didn't bother to negotiate a more optimal meeting date when I wouldn't feel pressured to squeeze it in. When the client recommended the date, I didn't think to propose an alternative, even though I'd seen my schedule that week and knew that I'd be bouncing coast to coast. I should have had the foresight to say, "You know, that week is just tough for my team and me. How about the following week?" By not minding my boundaries and applying the disciplines I had carefully developed as a professional, I set myself up for failure. Now I'm grateful I was able to learn from this experience, but, it really shouldn't have happened in the first place.

Sure, I could have easily chalked this massive blunder up to my hectic work schedule. "You know, I was just *so* busy," people say today in what seems to have become a common — and socially acceptable — excuse for poor performance. But I've grown to cringe when I hear this. First, look around — *everyone is busy*. Busyness isn't unique to anyone. Rather than tell people they're too busy, Sparks get to the heart of the matter by having a conversation with themselves about what's really going on:

- I'm late for the call because I didn't plan appropriately.
- I have no boundaries in life.
- I'm rescheduling on you (again) because this isn't a priority for me.
- I want you to feel sorry for me because I have so much to do.
- I don't know how to manage my time.
- This is the best excuse I've got for why I can't keep my commitments.

The only way to learn and grow as a Spark is to develop a sense of *accountability* for your actions. If you're so busy that your routine is killing your credibility with others and preventing you from being consistent, rather than blaming life for plotting against you, recognize that it's time to make some changes. A great place to start is with basic time management skills.

CREATING THE CAPACITY TO LEAD BY OWNING YOUR TIME

Time is the great equalizer. Every human being, no matter how successful, wealthy, or talented, has only 24 hours in a day. But what often differentiates high performers from the pack is what they do with the 1,440 minutes they're given each day. Unlike other resources, such as money or education, time is nonrenewable — you can't get more of it. All you can do is make the most of what you have. So protect your time like you do anything else that you value. You wouldn't walk into your place of employment and give your Visa card to your colleagues and ask them to spend away. So why, then, do we so freely give away our time when it's a critical variable in our performance equation?

Sparks need to learn how to "own" their time and invest in it wisely, which comes down to implementing time management disciplines. These simple, yet effective, practices allow you to create greater capacity in your life to lead yourself and others.

One of the most important time management skills we promote is maintaining white space in your calendar: setting aside a series of two- to three-hour blocks of time every week. Treat these open blocks as you would any other meeting or appointment. During these time blocks, think strategically, develop yourself professionally, or reach out to members of your network or mentors and invite them to lunch. White space is perfect for doing the key Spark activities you've identified as valuable for your life — especially the activities that will never be urgent but are extremely important.

By the way, white space isn't a time to catch up with your email — you should be doing that on a daily basis. But rather than react erratically to email, you need to respond to it more intentionally. We advocate responding to emails twice a day—at midmorning and in the late afternoon—so you can stay on top of your inbox and your emails don't overwhelm you. We've learned from experience that if every email is treated as a top priority, you wind up feeling like a dog on a choke collar being pulled in whatever direction its master wants it to go. Don't be that person. Direct your own time—don't have others direct it for you. Certainly, there are going to be days when you need to be more attentive and responsive to emails than others. But assess each email coming through for whether it needs a response *right now*—most emails are not emergencies.

Another key time management tip is to plan a realistic to-do list at the end of each business day. That's when you have the best perspective on what has to happen the next day to keep your success going. Make a realistic list of the two or three tasks that *must get done* the next day to keep moving forward on the initiatives you're undertaking. You're not compiling a wish list, but rather an "I'd better get these things done tomorrow or my credibility is going to suffer" list.

One final strategy we promote is a companion to the to-do list: doing the "worst first" when you arrive at work the next morning. Otherwise stated, start your day by doing the thing that you want to do *least* so you can get it out of your head the rest of the day. We often stress about things we don't want to do but have to do, like expense reports or proposal writing. Curiously, when we sit down and do them, they usually don't take as long as we expect. Eliminating these distractions early in the day frees us up mentally so we can be present for the rest of the day.

There are many more tricks to the time management trade, but we have found these three tactics to be game-changing for not only the professionals we work with but ourselves. Sometimes it's not doing more that allows you to be consistent. Sometimes it's developing the habit of doing less.

ONE LESS THING TO DO

Angie's Story

I have a highly optimistic, yet unrealistic, view of how much I can accomplish in a day. The fact that I can admit that means I'm close to getting a handle on my problem. I used to pack my days so tightly that my world would come undone if a telephone call went over five minutes or I encountered unexpected traffic on the way to a meeting.

The benefit of such a packed schedule is that you get to check a lot of things off your daily to-do list. The downfall is that there's a cost — you're always stressed about time, and you can't be fully mentally present for the activities you're engaged in. For example, when I went out to lunch, rather than being engrossed in the conversation I'd be distracted, always conscious of time. Or even on Saturdays at the beach, rather than giving myself over to family time I'd have this nagging "I should be doing something else" feeling. I found that being crazy busy was robbing me of all of life's joy. Suddenly my life was full of tasks that I had to move through instead of experiences I could find value in. I also found that my constant quest for more things to do was compromising my credibility — I was unable to give my best to whatever was in front of me, and what's worse, I was becoming very inconsistent with myself and others.

My problem didn't happen overnight. It started when I first had a home office and realized I could work as much as I wanted. I love what I do, so I didn't mind breaking from the mold of traditional working hours to keep up with projects and explore new initiatives. Then, as I found more success, others reached out to ask me to join committees, attend meetings, and participate in forums. It was fun traveling to different sites, meeting with professionals, and contributing as best I could. As my life and business developed and kids became a part of the equation, things got busier and my life became more dynamic. And then I had the crazy idea of going to grad school, which was the straw that finally broke the camel's back.

It wasn't the curriculum of grad school that drove me nuts. It was the time it took to keep up with classes while staying on top of Lead Star work, attempting to be an engaged mom, and settling into a new community. (My husband had just retired from the Marine Corps, and we had recently moved to northern Michigan.) There was so much change going on, and there were too many competing priorities. I couldn't keep up. I started scheduling meetings, then asking to reschedule at the last minute because something else popped up. I kept canceling coffee dates with new friends because something more pressing came along. Even my "therapy," otherwise known as my morning jog, didn't feel relaxing — jogging felt like a nuisance because I was doing it when I had other more pressing things that needed to get done. If I was consistent at anything, it was at being inconsistent. I wasn't living up to the Spark standards I promote, and what's worse, I was letting myself and others down.

I remember picking up Greg McKeown's book *Essentialism: The Disciplined Pursuit of Less* during this time — we had just featured him in one of Lead Star's Leadership Conversations, and his work really spoke to me. His book offered a perspective that I had never considered before. Rather than doing more, *what if I tried to do less?* I started to imagine what it would feel like to be less busy, and, honestly, it felt like a dream.

Confronting my reality wasn't difficult. The hard part was undoing what I had already done. The first step I took was to see what, exactly, I could let go of, which I knew wasn't going to be easy. I began by reviewing the past two weeks of my calendar to see which activities I'd engaged in that had not been connected to a goal or a priority. There were several to choose from — meetings I attended that didn't connect to work, lunch dates I accepted that could have waited until less busy times, projects that should have been delegated to team members.

The next step was making some tough decisions about what I was going to stop doing and, more importantly, what I wasn't going to start doing. After bowing out of a community group I had just joined and canceling a few meetings, I reached out to a board I served on and asked for a leave of absence while I finished grad school. I then started to enlist support from Lead Star's executive director, Liz, to help me stop taking on more projects. Whenever I'd get a new request, rather than instinctively saying yes right away, I'd give Liz a call to talk it through. Even my husband played along. I remember sitting in church one day listening to our pastor talk about all the volunteer opportunities open to members. They all sounded so fulfilling, especially building a house for Habitat for Humanity. I took out my bulletin and starting filling out the volunteer form. My husband snatched the paper out of my hand, shook his head, and whispered, with a smile, "Angie, get real." (He filled out the form for himself instead.)

I then started to create some rules for myself that turned out to be very useful — they helped me manage my "too quick to say yes" impulse. I decided that if I was going to give my time, it would only be to support certain causes I truly cared deeply about. I also decided that before I said yes to anything, I'd first think about it for twenty-four hours.

This rule prepared me for when people approached me to ask for my help. Rather than saying yes immediately, I started to say, "Let me get back to you." This bought me some time to think things through and then later deliver a carefully contemplated reply: "I can't right now." I also administered the HBU test every day — *Is what I'm doing at this moment the highest, best use of my time?* I was shocked at first by how many times the answer was no. But I started to improve over time.

Throughout this simplification process, what surprised me most was how tight a grip I had on my activities, as if being busy was a badge of honor I wore. When I'd travel for work and talk with clients about the challenges of my "one less thing to do" pursuit, it was very comforting to find out I wasn't alone. Other people agreed that doing more isn't better, but that for some strange reason it's very addictive. And not in a good way.

One woman I spoke with told me that she didn't realize she had a problem with always doing more until she paid attention to the negative dialogue going on in her mind. She confessed that she used to be one of those classic working parents who feed their kids meals in the car as they hurriedly shuttle them around between school and after-school activities. One day when she was dropping her kids off at an event, she noticed other moms in the parking lot laughing and having a good old time. They also were wearing tennis skirts and yoga pants, as if they were preparing to work out together. Her first thoughts were resentful. *Look at them! Not a care in the world and more time than they know what to do with!*

But then she stopped and asked herself, *Do you really resent them? Or do you envy them because they're so carefree and have time to socialize and do fun things together?* It was difficult for her to admit to herself at first, but it was indeed envy, not resentment, that she was feeling. She then thought long and hard about why she wasn't having fun and why she couldn't squeeze some joy out of her life. It wasn't due to her work schedule. She had a great employer that gave her a lot of flexibility. She was her own biggest barrier: she was the one who was overtasking and overscheduling herself. She wasn't happy, her husband wasn't happy, and it was becoming clear that her kids weren't happy either. When she made some conscious choices to dial down her activities, she quickly discovered that she could carve out time in her life, which she now fiercely protects because she has more time just to "be."

Another client shared how his busyness had a significant impact on the team he had been building carefully. He had spent a tremendous amount of time hiring the right people for the team positions, but once they landed the job he didn't have the time to nurture and develop them. He found that whenever he called his team members, their conversations weren't "real"; rather, they were always task-related. He knew he was managing his business because things were getting done on time, but what he failed to consider at the time was that he wasn't leading his team.

This became evident one day when one of his top performers dropped a resignation letter on him. He was stunned and surprised. "Why?" he asked her. "I just don't feel like this company cares about me," she replied. This was his wake-up call. He knew what she really meant. "I just don't feel like *you* care about me." He knew he had to make some changes because, if this employee felt like this, others did too.

He started by reorganizing his schedule to build more leadership time into his workweek. He stopped attending meetings that didn't move the business forward. He also made a point of implementing "stay interviews" with his team members — periodic check-ins to ensure that they were happy and weren't searching for new opportunities. By doing fewer things and spending more time on his relationships with his team, he was able to pull everyone together to work more cohesively and experience greater camaraderie.

By having *less* to do, Sparks discover that they can give more to the priorities they've already selected for themselves — at work, at home, and everywhere in between. They also find the time to rejuvenate themselves, which is a necessary aspect of high performance. Life's aha! moments don't happen as you hurriedly shift from task to task. They occur when you're relaxed and have the space to think broadly and clearly. Downtime is also an important time to reflect and assess how you're doing in living up to your own expectations of yourself — *Am I fulfilling my Spark potential? If not, what is getting in the way?*

Consistency and busyness are not the same thing. In fact, they are incompatible. If you are overworked, stressed, and clearly not performing at your best throughout the day, there is no way you are demonstrating consistency. The answer is to scale back on the many roles you've assumed and obligations you've signed up for. Better to be consistently top-notch at several tasks rather than weak, or terrible, at many. Being overcommitted doesn't allow you to behave like the Spark you can be.

SPARK ACTIONS

Developing consistency is a discipline that requires constant commitment. To build the habit of consistency:

- Assess your current state of readiness. Do you have the space to respond to whatever happens rather than merely react?
- Recognize your limits before your credibility and reputation suffer. You can do *any*thing, but you can't do *every*thing and be successful.
- Having "less to do" makes you more available for what matters most — at work and in life.

CHARGING AHEAD

Your reputation as a Spark isn't earned in one singular moment; it's earned in many moments over time. While you can never prevent the surprises and curveballs that life throws at you, you can manage yourself and your time, and doing this is critical to generating and maintaining consistency as well as keeping the commitments you make to yourself and to others. Consistency is the difference between a one-hit wonder and someone who has lasting success. It's the necessary quality that builds your reputation as a predictable, steady performer.

We're here to help you build more discipline into your work routine by providing the following resources on www.sparks lead.us:

- *The Consistency Habit:* Does your schedule allow you to be consistent? This exercise lets you reflect on your true priorities and gives you guidance on making them more present in your life. There are also tips on identifying activities you should stop doing so you can be more focused on the activities most important to you.
- *Time Management:* We all have periods when we have more to do than time to do it in. If this feels like an everyday experience to you, however, this resource will help you incorporate time management planning into your routine.

Once you're through with reflecting on these activities, you'll be in position to take the final step in your Spark journey: inspiring more Sparks.

CONCLUSION

As we hope you've discovered while reading *Spark*, leadership isn't a set of abstract concepts reserved only for those who are anointed "management material." Anyone can be a leader. *Spark* outlines seven essential behaviors you can develop that will lead you toward the better future you envision. Leadership development takes effort, commitment, and focus. But there's a return on your investment.

Being a Spark allows you to:

- Become aware of your values and more capable of ensuring that they're active in your life
- Earn trust and credibility in all your relationships
- Be accountable for missed expectations so that you can then work to be a part of the solution
- Imagine your future and take intentional actions toward it
- Develop a sense of team and camaraderie within the groups you're a part of
- Approach challenges and setbacks as well as new opportunities confidently
- Demonstrate consistency, which will help you keep your energy high and your focus set

Armed with the right knowledge and poised with the right mindset, you're ready to act. But our next question is: *Are you going to stop there?*

Now that you know the behaviors that will allow you to develop trust, have influence, and provide inspiration, what will you do to help others Spark too?

INSPIRING MORE SPARKS

While reading *Spark,* you probably had the thought occasionally that your own working world would be much more productive if others demonstrated leadership behaviors. Imagine what it would feel like if your team members solved problems *before* escalating them, took initiative *before* being asked, and communicated effectively *before* issues spun out of control.

We firmly believe that Sparks have a responsibility to expand their influence and to develop leaders in their midst. This makes teams more engaged, divisions run more efficiently, and organizations perform at a much higher level. Leadership development also facilitates talent development. Younger generations of workers are increasingly charged with greater responsibility than previous generations. The surest way for them to succeed is to have the competency and capacity to manage those responsibilities. Your active role in others' development guarantees both.

When we left active duty, we appreciated that the military equipped us with the intangibles — the leadership skills that would be invaluable to us in the private sector. Once we started working in the private sector, we didn't keep those skills a secret. We wanted our colleagues to share in our understanding of leadership — the Spark behaviors — because we knew that these skills are linked to success. We also created Lead Star because we saw an opportunity to promote this knowledge with a broader audience. We realized that if more professionals were introduced to leadership fundamentals, they'd experience more success in their approach to work and life.

We've met many Sparks since then who have similar motivations and goals. These men and women want to share leadership development with the teams they're a part of, whether that's an accounting department, a small to midsize business, a sales division, or a segment within a large enterprise. In truth, most of our introductions to organizations don't start with a human resources connection, where leadership development functions are typically housed. They begin with individuals who envision how they could achieve better results if only leadership skills were better represented in their organization.

What eventually ensues is a collaborative effort with HR and other key stakeholders to begin supporting talent development. Our role is to help organizations think differently about leadership development; we're not offering a class, but a cultural shift that takes will and commitment. While programming typically begins in the classroom, the responsibility is then placed on our clients and on us to create context for Sparks to emerge. We also challenge individuals to seek experiences that will help them experiment with and build Spark behaviors.

Our approach to program development has evolved to keep pace with our clients' needs. We're always seeking ways to be relevant, which is why we don't have a stock or standard "course." Our client engagements don't begin with us presenting a class list and a pencil to our clients and asking them to order up courses, like they're ordering from a sushi menu. Rather, every engagement starts with our cultural immersion in the client's organization so that we get to know the client. We've visited the manufacturing floors during the midnight shift in Denver, spent a few days in "man camp" on the North Slope in Alaska, and observed procedures in operating rooms with physicians. We do whatever it takes to really understand how leadership is expressed in the client's work.

We then meet with our client to have a dialogue about where hidden leadership opportunities exist. This meeting not only helps shape our curriculum but also gives us a real sense of how we can add value to the organization.

Our next step is democratizing leadership, which is our way of saying: we make leadership development accessible to everyone. We begin our programs by introducing leadership fundamentals to every employee, regardless of their development stage or their place on an organizational chart. How we do this is unique to each of our clients, but it can include a three-hour open enrollment course, a two-day classroom experience, or a series of webinars. We then create engagement opportunities for those who are truly interested, motivated, and committed to developing their leadership skills. This is the forge from which Sparks begin to emerge.

Through this process, we observe which employees are engaged and which employees are more passive in their approach to learning. Our goal is never to convert the passive learners — there are always going to be individuals in organizations who aren't growth-oriented. Instead, our aim is to help find the hidden gems — those individuals who might not have been selected for high-potential or emerging leaders programs — and then connect them with opportunities within the organization. In short, we want these Sparks to ignite. The best way to lead a change initiative or launch a new process or system is to get Sparks involved early and then give them the freedom to influence, direct, and guide others.

We then work with clients to transition all curricula to the organization for future delivery by in-house leaders. Leadership programs work best when organizational leaders step up and deliver them. This not only reinforces authenticity and relevancy but also spurs faster adoption throughout the organization.

As we get to know our clients well, we walk closely with them to assist and support them in identifying and developing their Sparks. We then step back slowly as the leadership culture takes hold within their organization.

Leader-led, peer-led, and employee-led programs are the future. It's the best way to ensure that managers are aligned with their company's cultural initiatives and that every leader is engaged in the leadership dialogue.

Ironically, this is surprisingly similar to how we were trained in the military. There is no such thing as an HR department in the armed forces. HR is everywhere. Everyone is a keeper of the culture. Everyone is prepared to mentor and to coach leadership development. That's an important lesson to be learned. Plus, blending operations with leadership helped us learn, grow, and develop at a much faster rate.

THE LEADERSHIP IMPERATIVE

Leadership at all levels isn't *just* an effective cultural strategy that organizations can adopt. It has now become a strategic imperative in today's world.

When tech companies have greater market caps than businesses with physical assets, like large hotel chains and retail department stores, it's clear that people, not just things, create organizational value. And when businesses have more to do with fewer resources, they need creative, innovative leaders who are willing to approach challenges as Sparks — people who think about what they *can* do, not what they *can't* do, to achieve results.

Any organization that is committed to its people and truly willing to invest the time and resources can adopt Spark behaviors. An ounce of leadership development can leverage all the technical and skills-based training your firm's been investing in. You can be a catalyst for this.

You now have the opportunity and the blueprint to shape how leadership is experienced in your environment. The small actions you take today can initiate a leadership movement in your organization. In short, you can spark change.

You're also not in this alone. We're here to help, and we're committed to continuing the dialogue on www.sparkslead.us. If you share in our conviction that Better Leaders = Better World, then let's roll up our sleeves and get started.

ACKNOWLEDGMENTS

Spark wouldn't have been possible without each of us having had the privilege to serve in the military. We're proud of our service and eternally grateful to have learned leadership from America's finest leaders. Since our time in uniform, we've had the opportunity to meet many other great leaders whose influence is also represented in our work.

We'd like to extend a special thanks to Esmond Harmsworth and Rick Wolff, who have been integral throughout *Spark*'s development. We also appreciate Marcia Layton Turner's efforts and guidance. We'd like to thank our spouses — Matt, Patrick, and Vera — and children — Judge, Gardner, Kara, Jessica, Brady, Connor, and Caitlin — for your patience while we collaborated together. Our families give us infinite sources of inspiration. You're the reason we Spark.

We also are eternally grateful to our team: Liz Lamirand, Laura Salapka, Jim Wyckoff, Patrick Lynch, Lisa Rohrer, Jena Persico, Patrick Nelson, and Jenn Terry. What can we say? You all are amazing! Thank you for your contributions to *Spark,* as well as for taking the helm on many firm initiatives while we hunkered down to write.

INDEX